CONTENTS

LEWIS CARROLL IN WONDERLAND
THE LIFE AND TIMES OF ALICE AND HER CREATOR

Stephanie Lovett Stoffel

"…the Rabbit actually *took a watch out of its waistcoat-pocket,* and looked at it.…"

DISCOVERIES®
HARRY N. ABRAMS, INC., PUBLISHERS

"Then what a bawling and a tearing of hair there will be! Pigs and babies, camels and butterflies, rolling in the gutter together—old women rushing up the chimneys and cows after them—ducks hiding themselves in coffee-cups, and fat geese trying to squeeze themselves into pencil cases. At last the Mayor of Leeds will be found in a soup plate covered up with custard, and stuck full of almonds to make him look like a sponge cake that he may escape the dreadful destruction of the Town."

Letter to Charles Dodgson from his father,
6 January 1840

CHAPTER 1
FROM ISLAND-FARM TO DREAMING SPIRES

Left: Charles Lutwidge Dodgson with a camera lens, 1863, photographed by O. G. Rejlander. Right: the Mad Tea-party, a color illustration by John Tenniel for *The Nursery Alice*.

A Cheshire childhood

All Saints' Church in the tiny village of Daresbury, England, was the first appointment for the young cleric Charles Dodgson, newly married to his first cousin Frances (Fanny) Lutwidge. A brilliant and diligent man, he had won a double first-class degree in classics and

mathematics at Christ Church, Oxford, and in an era of theological controversy he took firm stands in his much-admired sermons, several volumes of which were published. In time Dodgson (pronounced "Dodson") became canon of Ripon and then arch-deacon of Richmond.

But back in 1827 the Dodgsons found themselves in the Cheshire country-side, where they immediately began to fill their rural parsonage with children. Eventually this rollicking company was to include eleven siblings, seven girls and four boys, all of whom lived to old age. The third child and first son was born on 27 January 1832, five years before Queen Victoria came to the throne of England. He was named Charles Lutwidge Dodgson, but over a century and a half later he is known around the world as Lewis Carroll.

The man who invented Wonderland thus grew up in a large and well-established family, deep in the English countryside, and came of age together with the Victorian era. Rural Daresbury was a serene place; Charles later referred in verse to "An island-farm, mid seas of corn / Swayed by the wandering breath of morn— / The happy spot where I was born." Even when the boy was not at liberty to climb trees and play with frogs, his childhood was idyllic. The Dodgson household seemed made to order for this bright and sensitive child.

His mother was, by all contemporary reports, unfailingly patient and gentle. She delighted in her

Left: Charles Dodgson, Sr., as a young man (date unknown). Both he and his grandfather, the bishop of Elphin, who was also Frances's grandfather, shared the family gift of humor. Young Charles's parents were first cousins.

James McNeill Whistler, *Harmony in Green and Rose: The Music Room*, 1860–61. Victorian culture painted the family in rosy colors, but Dodgson's seems to have been truly warm and loving.

children, closely oversaw their education, and radiated the love that made her adored in her family. She doted on her eldest son, supervising his religious reading, worrying about his health, and providing him with a high—in his view almost divine—standard for human love.

Young Charles thrived under his father's hand as well. All the qualities of spiritual and administrative leadership that made Charles Dodgson, Sr., so effective a minister—for example, he created a chapel on a barge in order to bring the church to river people who could not come to it—were manifest in his household, where daily prayers were held and Sundays were strictly observed. Under his benign dictatorship, his children acquired self-discipline, a sense of duty, an education, and a powerful faith. He tutored his son in mathematics, classics, and literature, and one family anecdote has a very small Charles bringing him a book of logarithms and saying "Please explain!" This conscientious father seems to have been a continuous presence in his children's lives, despite his many professional duties, charities, and private studies.

Queen Victoria with her children, around 1865: representing the ideal mother.

The wide world

When Charles was 11 his father was appointed to St. Peter's Church in Croft, Yorkshire. The family took up residence in Croft Rectory in 1843, enjoying larger quarters, a town with amenities and other educated people, and an increased income. Before the family moved in, some remodeling was done to install a new floor in the nursery. A century later, in 1950, when the house was again remodeled, a curious cache was discovered under the floor. Apparently the Dodgson children had hidden away a kind of time capsule of treasures, including such items as a child's handkerchief, a penknife, bits of china, a small thimble, and a child's white glove. On a block of wood was inscribed, in what appears to be Charles's hand, this evocative verse: "And we'll wander through / the wide world / and chase the buffalo."

Although his studies were becoming increasingly serious, Charles was still a boy at Croft, with a boy's taste for games. It was here that he invented a backyard railway game, mainly for the pleasure of the burlesque rules by which it operated. Any passenger so unfortunate as to be derailed was required to allow at least three trains to run over him before qualifying for medical attention. His ever-expanding complement of siblings—the last born a year after the move—was Charles's first audience, and with them he developed the skills and love for entertaining children that were to make him happy throughout his life. There were parlor games of all sorts, puppet shows and plays, conjuring performances, and stories. The boy who dreamed up games with his siblings, mainly sisters, was to become a man who delighted in challenging the minds of bright young girls with puzzles and diverting them with stories.

Commemorative postage stamps from the island of Tristan da Cunha. The large image is based on an undated photograph by Dodgson of his family at Croft Rectory. His younger brother Edwin became a missionary to Tristan da Cunha, an isolated British protectorate in the South Atlantic Ocean.

"He will not rest satisfied without a most exact solution of whatever appears to him obscure."

At age 12 Charles went to Richmond School in the market town of Richmond, only ten miles away. The school had an excellent reputation: it was small and domestic, and Charles was able to board in the home of the headmaster. Stuart Dodgson Collingwood, his nephew and first biographer, says of Charles's Richmond days that he was known as a champion of the weak, and though "it is hard for those who have only known him as

A 19th-century engraving of the town of Richmond, in Yorkshire. Doubtless the schoolboys climbed, explored, and played knights in the ruins of its Norman castle.

B elow: the church and school in Richmond in 1821. The Richmond Grammar School appears to date to the fourteenth century and was refounded in 1567. This building stood from 1815 to 1850. Charles's headmaster, James Tate, was cheerful and kind, and Charles thrived there.

the gentle and retiring don to believe it, it is nevertheless true that long after he left school his name was remembered as that of a boy who knew well how to use his fists in defense of a righteous cause."

Charles excelled in mathematics and classics. His headmaster, a Mr. Tate, told the Dodgsons that their son's schoolwork showed "a very uncommon share of genius" and that he was uncompromising "where important faith or principles are concerned," but "exceedingly lenient towards lesser frailties." This was an essential characteristic of Charles's throughout his life: an unbending adherence to the prime principles of life, coupled with a loving tolerance for human imperfection.

After two terms at Richmond, in January 1846 he moved on to studies at Rugby, a prestigious school in central England, and his childhood idyll ended. The oldest boys organized the extracurricular life of the school, and for the majority of students this meant suffering a good deal of institutionalized bullying and harassment. Pranks, teasing, and humiliations were common.

The work was demanding, and Charles excelled in all his subjects, usually bringing home a prize at the end of the term. Divinity and mathematics were clearly his strong subjects, and his parents received letters of praise from his teachers and the headmaster. Documentation from Charles himself about his unpleasant experiences is scarce; he would not have wanted to alarm his family with tales of his unhappiness. However, he wrote a decade later: "I cannot say that I look back upon my life at a Public School with any sensations of pleasure, or that any earthly considerations would induce me to go through my three years again."

The youthful writer: family magazines

During his school years Charles organized a series of Dodgson family magazines. The first of these, *Useful and Instructive Poetry,* was composed entirely by him during a

Above left: the interior of the school chapel. At Rugby the boys were regularly uplifted and improved spiritually by sermons here, but largely left to their own devices to put good advice into practice.

Above: an illustration by Arthur Hughes from Thomas Hughes's 1857 novel *Tom Brown's School Days,* set at Rugby. The artist later became a friend of Dodgson, who purchased one of his paintings, *The Lady with the Lilacs* (now in the Art Gallery of Ontario, Toronto), in 1863.

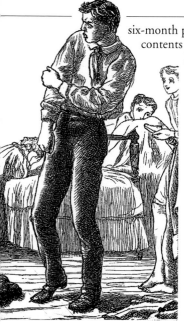

six-month period at Richmond. Its contents include a poem about a headstrong man who, like the later Humpty Dumpty, refuses to come down from a high wall; several limericks; a Shakespeare parody; and a number of mock-serious didactic poems, with morals such as *Never stew your sister* and *You mustn't.* These early examples of his fluency, dry wit, and facility with parody are neatly written.

The Rectory Magazine dates from the Rugby period and represented the efforts of his entire family. There are serialized stories, essays with such titles as "Reasonings on Rubbish" and "Things in General," and a section called "Answers to Correspondents." No questions appear, but the answers include "We think not, at least

Arthur Hughes, *Home from Work,* 1861. Warmhearted, sentimental Victorian scenes of family life were among Charles Dodgson's favorite paintings in adulthood; perhaps they reminded him of his own happy childhood.

Below: children enjoy reading in an early Victorian scene.

Left: the diversions of *The Rectory Umbrella* shield the reader from the perils of boredom and peevishness in this undated drawing by Dodgson. Its stories, poems, and essays twinkle with high irony and deadpan Carrollian humor.

A *Man and His Scroll,* Dodgson's undated illustration for his Gothic melodrama *The Walking-Stick of Destiny,* serialized in *The Rectory Umbrella.*

as far as regards snails and turpentine," "Perhaps," "Yes: for instance a brass shoe-horn," and "Round the rugged rocks the ragged rascals ran." This last suggests that exercises to correct a family tendency to stutter or stammer were under way. (Charles had a stammer, which he called a "hesitation.") Charles's serial "Sidney Hamilton" is a perceptive parody of the flowery, melodramatic popular fiction of the day, complete with overblown descriptions of ludicrous events and contrived characters— bandits, a disowned son, and a case of mistaken identity.

The family's contributions to the magazines waned gradually, and the next significant one is entirely Charles's work. *The Rectory Umbrella* was written in his late teens and college years. Here, as in his later writing, he loves to explore ideas that are logical in principle but absurd in practice. One essay proves that a stopped clock is preferable to one that loses a minute a day, since at least the stopped clock is correct twice a day, while the other is never accurate. His parodies have become more mature and sophisticated, and have acquired ridiculous, straight-faced footnotes. An essay entitled "Difficulties No. 1" asks the question: at what point in circling the globe does one move from one date to the next? He took up this topic again in an 1860 lecture to the Ashmolean Society at Oxford, called "Where Does the Day Begin?" The question was answered only in 1884, with the establishment of the International Date Line.

THE SPELL.

From a window thrown,
To the ground he fell.
Yet he brake no bone,
He's alive and well!
And the poisoned sip
Of the offered cup,
Hath missed his lip,
He hath ta'en no sup!
Yet, Signor, beware,
Thou shalt rue!
There is much to dare,
There is much to do!
The time comes quick,
When thou shalt see,
The Wall

STUDIES FROM ENGLISH POETS Nº III

"He gave it to his father."   Ossian.

His last family magazine, *Mischmasch*, created between 1855 and 1862, is the work of a young adult. Along with humorous essays, poems, and parodies, it includes some serious work, clippings of published pieces, burlesque etiquette rules, and a maze. Several of

TWAS BRYLLYG, AND Yᴱ SLYTHY TOVES
DID GYRE AND GYMBLE IN Yᴱ WABE:
ALL MIMSY WERE Yᴱ BOROGOVES;
AND Yᴱ MOME RATHS OUTGRABE.

Above: an undated comic drawing by Dodgson of a man with a club, from *Mischmasch*. Left: this undated "Stanza of Anglo-Saxon Poetry" and its scholarly exposition appeared in *Mischmasch*. One of Dodgson's several burlesques of Old English, it is an early version of the first stanza of "Jabberwocky." Note the runic-style handwriting.

the poems were republished much later in a book he entitled *Phantasmagoria* and "She's All My Fancy Painted Him" underwent a sea-change and appeared in the trial of the Knave of Hearts in *Alice in Wonderland.*

Above: Peckwater Quad, and below, Tom Quad of Christ Church. Dodgson resided in both at different times.

He finds his place at Christ Church

Christ Church, at Oxford University, was not the ideal place for a promising student of mathematics—the vanguard in that subject was at Cambridge—but it was unquestionably prestigious and academically distinguished, and it was the college of Charles's father. Following Rugby, Charles matriculated at Oxford in May 1850, though he did not begin his studies there until January 1851, and he returned home a mere two days later, when his mother unexpectedly died. Her younger, unmarried sister Lucy assumed management of the household.

College in Dodgson's time was both more rigorous and less structured than it is today. While many students took their studies seriously, others merely pursued youthful pleasures and sports. Pranks and practical jokes abounded, and at times student celebrations or protests grew into genuine, destructive riots. However, some came to Christ Church for the rigorous education it had provided to many of the greatest clerics, scholars, and statesmen of the land. Charles Dodgson was among these.

He fell into the college routine of morning chapel and evening meals, and a long sequence of examinations to obtain his degree. Newly independent, he went to London in the summer of 1851 for the Great Exhibition at the Crystal Palace. The following summer he visited the London home of his uncle Skeffington Lutwidge, his mother's brother. Uncle Skeffington shared his love of gadgets, puzzles, wonders, and abstractions. Together they passed many pleasant hours with microscopes and telescopes, and it was Uncle Skeffington who introduced Charles to his great lifelong avocation, photography.

The interior of Christ Church Cathedral, where Dodgson attended daily services.

The Crystal Palace in 1851, at the time of the Great Exhibition, the first world's fair.

Toward the end of 1852 Charles received first-class honors in mathematics. This achievement and his general good reputation brought him a reward that marked a great milestone in his life: he was appointed to a Studentship. This was a prestigious scholarly award and an unusual distinction for an undergraduate. Corresponding to a fellowship at other colleges, a Studentship entitled its

A pensive young Charles Dodgson in 1855.

holder to a small stipend and the right to remain in residence at Christ Church for life. The term *Student* thus referred to a senior member of the university. Many Students, such as the elder Charles Dodgson, held a Studentship for only a few years before proceeding with their careers, since the award stipulated that one enter holy orders and remain unmarried. Yet it carried no other obligations, and a student might teach or pursue research as he pleased. In Charles's case, the Studentship conferred on him a comfortable situation that was to suit him for life. In 1853 he began to keep a diary, a habit he maintained throughout his life. His diaries remain a primary source of information and some insight into his character and thought. He was a punctilious and detailed diarist, but was always a reserved man and revealed little of his deepest feelings or anxieties. By the end of 1854 he had completed the last examinations for his bachelor's degree.

Dodgson's 1868 sketch of himself is from a verse letter to a little girl named Maggie Cunnynghame and is labeled, "What I Look Like When I'm Lecturing."

Gladly would he learn and gladly teach

Charles began his teaching career in 1855; he was 23 years old. College positions were not as well-defined as they are today; a researcher or professor associated with Christ Church might be called up to perform a variety of functions. Charles became a tutor simply by taking on his first student. In a letter home he entertained his family with a tale in which scouts (an Oxford term for servants), tutor, and pupil are all equally mystified by the educational process:

My one pupil has begun his work with me, and I will give you a description how the lecture is conducted. It is the most important point, you know, that the tutor should be *dignified,* and at a distance from the pupil, and that the pupil should be as much as possible *degraded*— otherwise you know, they are not humble enough. So I sit at the further end of the room; outside the door (*which is shut*) sits

the scout; outside the outer door (*also shut*) sits the sub-scout; halfway down the stairs sits the sub-sub-scout; and down in the yard sits the *pupil*....The lecture goes on, something like this:

The upper floor of Christ Church Library in 1911. As sub-librarian Dodgson had an office here.

> *Tutor.* "What is twice three?"
> *Scout.* "What's a rice tree?"
> *Sub-scout.* "When is ice free?"
> *Sub-sub-scout.* "What's a nice fee?"
> *Pupil* (timidly). "Half a guinea!"
> *Sub-sub-scout.* "Can't forge any!"
> *Sub-scout.* "Ho for Jinny!"
> *Scout.* "Don't be a ninny!"
> *Tutor* (looks offended…)

As the spring progressed he took on more pupils, including a private arrangement to instruct a group of mathematics candidates. He was appointed sub-librarian, which increased his income. He had two hopes for the near future: to become the mathematical lecturer (that is, principal teacher of mathematics in the college) and to secure a mathematics scholarship. He chastised himself in his diary for wasting the term and falling behind in his work; nevertheless, in May he obtained another scholarship. The fledgling author also recorded progress on two mathematics works.

Before going home for the summer in 1855 Charles rewarded himself with another visit to London, where he viewed paintings at the Royal Academy, visited the Botanic Gardens, and attended Shakespeare plays, Rossini operas, and a scholarly lecture. At home he passed a pleasant and productive summer in reading and research, and honed his teaching skills at his father's parish school. He started *Mischmasch,* read the poetry of Tennyson and Coleridge, and visited relatives. By the end of 1855, which he recorded as the most eventful year of his life, he was back at Oxford. After some uncertainty, at age 24 he won the mathematical lectureship he sought and became a fully established member of the Christ Church community: university teacher, scholar, and author of sober treatises on mathematics.

The interior of a gallery at London's Victoria and Albert Museum in the late 19th century.

"You shall have the announcement of the last piece of good fortune this wonderful term has had in store for me, that is, a *1st class in Mathematics.*... I am getting quite tired of being congratulated on various subjects: there seems to be no end of it. If I had shot the Dean, I could hardly have had more said about it."

Letter to his sister Elizabeth,
9 December 1852

CHAPTER 2

OXFORD: THE LIFE OF THE MIND

Left: the Great Gate, the main entrance to Christ Church in a 1911 painting by Arthur Garratt. Right: the pretentious Frog-Footman and Fish-Footman from *Alice in Wonderland*. Dodgson's academic colleagues were occasionally equally self-important and sometimes found themselves the targets of his satiric wit.

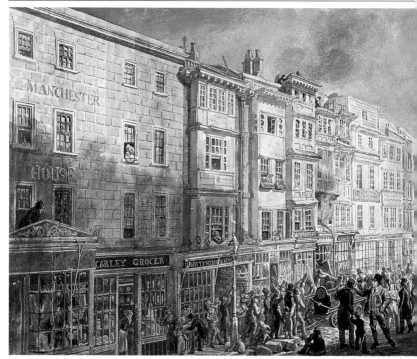

The man emerges

Dodgson was an easily recognizable figure as he strode about the Oxford streets and quadrangles. He was tall and was remembered as being even taller because he was so thin and carried himself ramrod straight. His clothes were of old-fashioned cut and he wore his wavy hair longer than was the prevailing style; even as a young man he had the bearing of a timeless Oxford don. The only change in his appearance over the years was the gradual graying of his hair. His thinness was due to an ascetic diet and his confirmed habit of taking long, brisk walks.

A childhood illness had left him deaf in his right ear, for which he compensated by always sitting to the right at the theater and staying to the right of walking companions. Dodgson and six of his sisters stammered in varying degrees, and he consulted several specialists in an attempt to manage and mitigate this awkward trait.

A bustling city street in 19th-century London. Oxford too had its lively streets of shops, and the young scholar loved both cities.

He once remarked that reading aloud caused him particular anxiety, since he could see a difficult word coming. As a result, he avoided reading lessons in church even more than delivering sermons.

The year he began to teach, 1855, was an important year for Christ Church as well. The old dean of the college died and his successor, Henry George Liddell, arrived. The dean of Christ Church was the head of both the college and Christ Church Cathedral, and a person of public importance. Liddell was already an eminent man: he had been headmaster of Westminster School and chaplain to Prince Albert. Tall, handsome, dynamic, and only 44, Liddell brought considerable charisma to the leadership of both college and cathedral. The influential art critic John Ruskin, a friend and colleague, praised Liddell's appearance, calling him "one of the rarest types of nobly presenced Englishmen," and admired his artistic ability and sensitivity. While his predecessor had been exceedingly conservative, Liddell was seen as an agent of reform, both religious and administrative. Change was in the air at Oxford, as it was throughout mid-Victorian England. Many traditions, such as the prohibition against married faculty, were being questioned as the university moved toward greater secularity.

Charles Dodgson's professional life was much affected by the arrival of Henry Liddell. As a

The authoritative academic Henry George Liddell in his early years as dean of Christ Church, in an 1858 drawing by George Richmond. Liddell, a distinguished scholar, was coauthor of the monumental *Greek-English Lexicon,* still today the standard reference work for ancient Greek.

conscientious member of Christ Church he participated
in debates concerning the various controversies raised by
the change in administration, and as a satirist
he was in green clover, producing quantities of
barbed and humorous pamphlets over the
years. But it was his personal life that was most
deeply affected by the appointment of the new
dean and the arrival of his large family. Liddell
had married the former Lorina Reeve, a dark
and regal beauty who became quite a presence
in Oxford. If Liddell was the most important
man at the university, his wife was surely the
most powerful woman, with tremendous
influence on its social life. Five children had
been born to the Liddells, but one son
had died in a scarlet-fever epidemic at
Westminster; at the time of the family's arrival
at the Deanery, the four remaining small
Liddells were Harry, Lorina, Alice, and Edith.
Four more children were born at Oxford: Rhoda in 1858,
Violet in 1864, Eric in 1865, and Lionel in 1868.

Lewis Carroll comes to life

With his own schooling behind him, the young don now
had the leisure to develop his wider interests and talents.
In the mold of the Victorian Renaissance man, he was
to hold several official positions—scholar, teacher of
mathematics and logic, member of the clergy—and
actively pursued his enthusiasm for the theater, the fine
arts, poetry, and storytelling, and a passion for the
fledgling art of photography.

In 1855 Dodgson contributed several pieces to the
small magazine *Comic Times,* published in London.
These were typical of his lighter writing: parodies, sets
of comical rules and instructions, a funny essay on
photography. *Comic Times* published only sixteen issues,
but in the same year the staff launched another humor
magazine, *The Train.* It was to *The Train*'s editor,
Edmund Yates, that Charles Dodgson submitted a list
of potential pseudonyms, so that he could preserve
his real name for the publication of his serious work.
Always a lover of anagrams, and amazingly adept at

them, he offered scrambled versions of his first two names, Charles Lutwidge: Edgar Cuthwellis and Edgar U. C. Westhill. He also reversed and adapted Charles Lutwidge to arrive at Louis Carroll and Lewis Carroll. Yates was asked to choose among them, and it is hard now to imagine his choosing other than as he did.

The poem "Solitude" marked the debut of Lewis Carroll. It was a mournful and rather treacly Victorian exercise, in which the speaker longs to be alone so that he can live in the past:

> I'd give all wealth that toil hath piled,
>   The bitter fruit of life's decay,
> To be once more a little child
>   For one short sunny day.

O pposite: Children of prosperous Victorian families often sat for portraits—more commonly painted than photographed.

I n Dodgson's comical and satiric short story "Novelty and Romancement," written for *The Train,* an over-eager, sentimental poet is thrilled to find romancement for sale, only to discover that the product in question is actually roman cement.

Carroll's contributions to the short-lived *Train* ran the gamut of his literary talents and reflected the full range of popular literature in the 1850s. Among the other sentimental pieces was one written in honor of Florence Nightingale, who only a few years earlier had won the admiration of the world with her heroic battlefield nursing in the Crimean War.

Dodgson's sense of humor and skeptical view of sentimentality are never long absent. In another poem, "Resolution and Independence," an early version of the White Knight's song in *Through the Looking-Glass,* he parodies the revered poet William Wordsworth.

But his best work in *The Train* was the poem "Hiawatha's Photographing." Metrically it is an inspired copy of the Longfellow poem "Hiawatha," but the subject is human vanity and the style wryly satiric. Members of a family sit one by one for a photographic portrait by the photographer Hiawatha, each with a clear notion of how he or she would like to be seen by others. The pictures all fail until a group portrait catches them together in a perfect, unflattering likeness.

In the poem "Hiawatha's Photographing" the son (left), influenced by the Oxford art theorist John Ruskin, strikes an aesthetic pose for his portrait. Above: Hiawatha behind his camera.

Dodgson placed poems in a few other periodicals as well. One of his serious poems, "Faces in the Fire," appeared in Charles Dickens's magazine *All the Year Round* and is another foray into nostalgic pathos. Maudlin sentiment is a recurrent theme in Dodgson's writing, sometimes sincere, often treated parodically. Not yet 30, he often wore the mask of weary middle age, donning with ease the mantle of the "Aged, Aged Man" (later brilliantly deconstructed in the figures of Father William in *Alice in Wonderland* and the White Knight in *Through the Looking-Glass*). Within a few years he had indeed begun to describe himself as an old man.

> **"From his shoulder Hiawatha took his camera of rosewood—made of sliding, folding rosewood—neatly put it all together"**

Dodgson was well able to bring his abundant levity to the trials and tribulations of the photographer. He purchased his first camera in 1856. At this time, photography was a complex, involved technology and it suited him for at least two powerful reasons. First, he took great pleasure in the many details, the fussy mechanics of making the cumbersome equipment and process work, and since there was plenty of room for innovation and refinement, he loved the freedom of play that this complicated chemistry afforded. Second, photography provided a unique, novel, and modern means of artistic expression. In love with art and never satisfied with his charming but amateurish

An 1883 illustration for Dodgson's tongue-in-cheek poem "A Sea Dirge," in which he describes the horrors of the seaside. In reality he adored the sea and passed many vacations at English coastal resorts.

draftsmanship, Dodgson found in photography the means by which he could realize his ideas about art and make the leap from gallery-goer to artist.

Collodion wet-plate photography became available to the public in 1855. To take a picture one had to polish a glass plate and coat it in a darkroom with a light-sensitive mixture of collodion and silver nitrate. The wet plate was then promptly exposed and immediately returned to the darkroom to be dried and varnished. The exposure required a lot of light, which meant using outdoor sunlight with a long exposure time—as much as forty-five seconds—during which the subject could not move or the image would blur or even vanish. Plein-air photography required the photographer to transport sixty to eighty pounds of equipment on an outing. One's hands were stained black by the chemicals, and practitioners of the "black art" (such as Dodgson and Julia Margaret Cameron) were well-known for always wearing gloves socially.

Although Dodgson photographed a few landscapes early in his career, his greater interest lay in portraiture. Because of his talent for entertaining and winning the trust of children, he is today considered the premier photographer of children of the Victorian era. His stories, games, and friendly interest in them brought relaxed and natural-looking children before the lens, compensating for the necessity that they remain absolutely still for the long exposure. Dodgson also had some success as a photographer of celebrities. In the early days of the camera the famous were not yet wary of being approached, and both the great and the obscure wanted their pictures taken. Dodgson was able to use photography as an entrée to Tennyson (among other notables), and felt that they were meeting as fellow artists.

A wet-plate camera, made between 1855 and 1880. After composing and focusing the image through the grid, upside down and backward, the photographer removed the grid and inserted the box containing the prepared glass plate, which he then exposed.

"I mark this day with a white stone"

On 25 April 1856 young Mr. Dodgson went with a borrowed camera to the Deanery to photograph Christ Church Cathedral. He had no luck with his pictures, but did find in the garden the three daughters of the dean. He had already met and befriended little Harry and Lorina, but this was his first encounter with Alice, then a week away from her fourth birthday. In his diaries

The three Liddell sisters in the Deanery garden, Christ Church, photographed by Dodgson in 1856.

Dodgson used the Roman poet Catullus's practice of figuratively marking a particularly wonderful day with a white stone. This was a white-stone day, as his diary records. Dodgson did not know then, as we do now, how important his friendship with Alice was to be, but he sensed something special about her from the first day.

This meeting, coupled with the purchase of his own camera equipment, launched a period of frequent comings and goings between Dodgson and the youthful occupants of the Deanery. There was much picture taking, as well as parlor games, stories, and boating picnics on the river, usually in the company of a governess. Ever conscious of her social status, Alice's mother was pleased to have her children photographed but at the same time anxious to keep Dodgson in his place. He was, after all, less important in the Oxford hierarchy than the Liddell family. As he became a regular visitor to the nursery, she made sure that his free and easy rapport with the children did not lead to assump-tions about his place at the Deanery. Their social relations through the years were punctuated by tensions, snubs, and estrangements; Dodgson maintained his complex professional relation-

Charles Dodgson at a nursery tea party with the Liddell children.

ship with the dean and his deep friendship with the children, and Mrs. Liddell strove to see that he received the minimum courtesy due his position, and no more.

Photography led the young man to places other than the Deanery. In 1857 he made a portrait of Tennyson's niece, Agnes Grace, dressed as Little Red Riding Hood. He visited the family more than once, dining with them and showing Tennyson his photo album, and he eventually photographed the poet and his sons. Over the next dozen years Dodgson maintained this acquaintance, getting on well with the boys, Lionel and Hallam.

Dodgson at first tried to make his hobby of photography pay for itself, and with this in mind he approached Ryman's, the Oxford picture dealer. While he was never by any means a commercial photographer, he did sell some costume and anatomical photos through Ryman's and, later in his career, some portraits, including Tennyson's. Yet his hobby was a private affair, inspired by his own passion for it and shared primarily with friends and family. While he went to numerous photographic exhibitions in London, at Ryman's, and elsewhere, he

Dodgson's 1857 photograph of Agnes Grace Weld as Little Red Riding Hood (above left) was his introduction to her uncle, the poet Alfred, Lord Tennyson (center), whom he also photographed that year, together with Tennyson's son Hallam (right).

displayed his own work only once. The Photographic Society of London exhibited four of his works, including *Little Red Riding Hood,* in 1858.

Dodgson's best-known photographs today are his remarkable, sensitive portraits of children. His delight in the company of children, especially little girls, has inevitably led to much speculation that his interest in

them was not entirely innocent. His photographs of them included some nudes, and though this was by no means an uncommon genre at the time, it is viewed today with some suspicion. The assumption is made that a bachelor's interest in little girls must be sexual, and that a photographer of little girls must be a voyeur. The usual clichés about repressed Victorian sexuality come into play in this all-too-common assessment of Dodgson's character. But to view him so is to judge him by the standards of our time, while taking no account of the culture in which he lived. Charles Dodgson grew up

Opposite: an American photographer of the Victorian period portrays a family's children in a pastoral idyll. Below right: Mary Cassatt's 1878 painting *Little Girl in a Blue Armchair.* Victorian painters as well as photographers made images of children with ambiguous undertones.

Beatrice Hatch by the sea in 1873, in a watercolor painted by Anne Lydia Bond, apparently by laying the watercolor paper over a print of Dodgson's photograph. When a little girl was happy to run around in her "favorite dress of nothing," and her mother consented, Dodgson on occasion took photographs of nude models. He was punctilious about the sensibilities of all involved, and took care that the pictures remained private. It was thought that all had been destroyed until four were found in the Rosenbach Collection and were published by Morton Cohen in 1978. Beatrice and her sister, Evelyn, were Dodgson's friends for years, and he photographed them often.

surrounded by sisters and was adept at the sort of play favored by girls of his time—stories, puzzles, and word games. He was a born teacher, and many of the pastimes he invented for his child-friends were designed to teach them to think. It thrilled him to see a young mind begin to grasp the workings of logic. Had he been a woman, perhaps his interest in the development of children and the joy he took in their fresh way of thinking would not seem so odd.

The romanticizing of childhood was part of the Victorian ethos. Dodgson, a devout Christian, saw children in Wordsworthian terms, as "trailing clouds of

Following pages: four portraits by Dodgson of child-friends: Evelyn Wilson-Todd, Beatrice Henley, Katie Brine, and Beatrice Hatch. His great sympathy for children and sensitivity to individual personalities give these vivid pictures their unique charm, and place him among the early masters of photography.

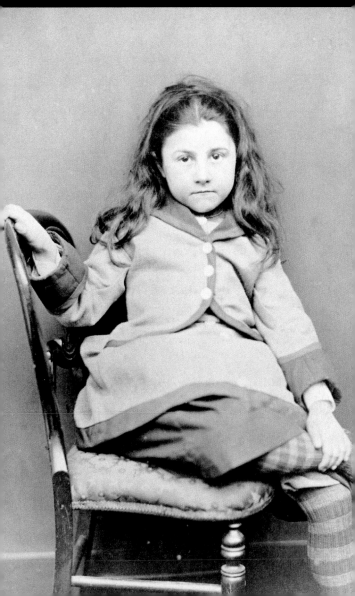

glory," freshly arrived from the presence of God, uncontaminated and asexual. For romantics such as he the company of children was a way to experience the state of humanity before the Fall, a whisper of Eden; and to a shy, clever man with a stutter, a complex mind, and

a quick, fanciful sense of humor, the companionship of children may have been a natural refuge.

As for his photographs, the study of the nude body has been the hallmark of serious artists for centuries, and Dodgson truly saw himself as an artist in his medium—as indeed he is seen today in every general history of photography. The adult nude was to him perhaps all too sexualized; the female child, whose body is not yet sexual, provided a way for the artist in him to celebrate the human form without obliging him to come to terms with humans as sexual beings. The nude child was a stock image in Victorian greeting cards and other commercial images, as well as among pioneering photographers. Julia Margaret Cameron, Alice Boughton, Frank M. Sutcliffe, and Thomas Eakins are only a few of the 19th-century artists who photographed nude children.

Dodgson's strong moral and religious convictions were nowhere more deeply felt than in his attitude toward sexuality. No doubt he was ill at ease with the sexual side of human life. The temper of the times aggravated and abetted his diffidence, and perhaps he experienced difficulties (sexual or otherwise) that no amount of posthumous psychoanalyzing can definitively pinpoint. He had many deep friendships with adult women, but

Left: Alice Boughton, *Children—Nude,* 1902, platinum print. The image of the nude child in much Victorian art signified sweet innocence, inspiration, or virtue.

Evelyn Hatch seated nude, an 1879 Dodgson photograph, hand-tinted by an unknown artist.

seems to have had no real romances or sexual liaisons with them. An unmarried man, apparently sexually inactive, is today seen as an oddity at best; it should be noted, however, that six of Dodgson's sisters also

remained unmarried, and that bachelorhood was, in academic life, well within the norm. We can never be sure if there was a sublimated sexuality mixed in with the intellectual and spiritual pleasures he derived from his friendships with young girls. But there is no evidence whatsoever that he made any sexual advances toward them. Not only would such behavior be contrary to everything we know about Dodgson—and indeed profoundly shocking to him— but the many tributes his child-friends paid him later in

Evelyn Hatch, reclining nude, another rare 1879 photograph by Dodgson, printed on emulsion on a curved piece of glass and overpainted in oil by an unknown hand.

Left: *Venus Chiding Cupid and Removing His Wings,* an 1872 photograph by the well-known photographer Julia Margaret Cameron, who often dressed her subjects as mythological or historical figures and whose nude image of a child here refers to Renaissance images of Cupid.

rfect propriety in their relations. From the
on's death in 1898 until the 1970s several
known as little girls published memoirs
in which they recalled their remarkable childhood friend
and described in warm terms how greatly they had
valued him. All were happy to speak openly of their
friendship with Dodgson; none declined to discuss him.

The theater—the art of life

Dodgson brought great intensity to his many interests:
he took his teaching and administrative duties in college
very seriously; he believed in the power of logic to solve
problems; he was punctilious in
his personal affairs; and he was
methodical, even obsessive, in his
record keeping. As for the theater, he
lost his heart to it. Like many another
stagestruck amateur, he became a
lifelong theater-goer, cultivated
theatrical friendships, and wrote on
and for the theater. He told stories
like an actor, using different voices,
and one child-friend, the actor Bert
Coote, later wrote that his sense of
theater was extraordinary.

In 1855, at age 23, he saw his first
staged Shakespeare, *Henry VIII*,
starring Charles Kean and Ellen Tree.
Dodgson was especially impressed
with the effect of angels descending
to the queen. "It was like a delicious
reverie," he wrote in his diary, "or the
most beautiful poetry. This is the true
end and object of acting—to raise the
mind above itself, and out of its petty
everyday cares…. So I could fancy (if
the thought be not profane) would
real angels seem to our mortal
vision." In later years he wrote again on the power of the
stage to express pure, inspiring, and elevating ideals.

In the summer of 1856 he saw *The Winter's Tale* in London
and in his diary especially admired the 9-year-old actress

The young Ellen Terry
(at right) in her
debut role as Mamillius
in *The Winter's Tale*, 1856.

John Everett Millais, *Ferdinand Lured by Ariel*, 1849. In an account of an 1857 production of *The Tempest* Dodgson praised "the concluding scene, where Ariel is left alone, hovering over the wide ocean, watching the retreating ship. It is an innovation on Shakespeare, but a worthy one, and the conception of a true poet." He adored both Shakespeare and Millais, one of the Pre-Raphaelite Brotherhood, a group of painters and poets devoted to an aesthetic of beauty and narrative, with a taste for romanticized medieval imagery and a dislike of the modern, industrialized England of their time.

Ellen Terry for her "remarkable ease and spirit." That winter he saw her again, as Puck in *A Midsummer Night's Dream.* Terry was to become the greatest actress of her time and one of Dodgson's dearest friends.

Shakespeare was not the young man's only fare. He enjoyed farces, melodramas, operas, and the other Victorian dramatic offerings popular at the time, but now mostly consigned to obscurity. Among these were the German Reed family's entertainments for audiences who did not consider the theater respectable. (Much later he considered them as producers for a staged *Alice in Wonderland.*) He attended and gave magic-lantern shows, public slide shows illustrating lectures or stories. Ballet he found unnatural and unpleasant. His diary shows clearly that he enjoyed comedies, if they were not vulgar; yet he reserved his lengthiest comments for serious theater, which was magical to him. A production

An art exhibition at the Royal Academy.

of Goethe's *Faust,* seen in Glasgow in 1857, led him to comment that the stage's ability to depict abstract ideas was all too powerful and, in a subject as horrifying as a man's transactions with the devil, could be misleading.

Below left: John Everett Millais photographed by Dodgson in 1865.

An empathy with the Pre-Raphaelites

London at the height of the Victorian era offered far more than theater. Music and art were to be found everywhere: he saw the great Swedish soprano Jenny Lind sing Handel's *Messiah;* galleries displayed

the latest trends in painting and sculpture. At the Royal Academy Exhibition in the summer of 1855 he saw a work by the English Pre-Raphaelite painter Sir John Everett Millais and in his diary called it the finest picture there. Dodgson read a book on the movement in the spring of 1857 and that summer met the Pre-Raphaelite painter Holman Hunt. Later he published a poem inspired by Hunt's *The Finding of the Saviour in the Temple.*

At the Royal Academy Exhibition in July he again enjoyed Millais's works. At the Edinburgh National Gallery that fall he admired Sir Joseph Noël Paton's picture of Oberon and Titania from *A Midsummer Night's Dream;* he counted 165 fairies in the painting! Throughout his life he was drawn to the glowing and meticulous Pre-Raphaelite paintings that so beautifully

William Holman Hunt poses for Dodgson, probably in the 1860s.

Holman Hunt's masterful painting *The Finding of the Saviour in the Temple* was one of Dodgson's favorite works of art. He loved its lush decorative detail, dramatic presence, and religious sincerity.

Sir Joseph Noël Paton,
*The Reconciliation of
Oberon and Titania,* 1847.
Dodgson's fascination
with this charming
painting can be readily
understood: its whimsy
and sweetness capture all
that is most lighthearted
in Shakespeare's play, and
it depicts fairyland as a
benign and amusing
place. One may imagine
him standing before it,
counting up the precise
number of its fairies—the
mathematician and the
fantasist in him equally
entertained.

A marvelous, dense scene of fairyland by the eccentric Richard Dadd, *The Fairy Feller's Masterstroke,* is perhaps less blithe and sunny than Paton's. Images of fairyland abounded in Victorian art and appealed greatly to Dodgson.

In his 1861 pamphlet on an Oxford University controversy, the proposed endowment of a professorship, Dodgson is perhaps more amused by the proposal's thorny and academic wording than interested in its politics.

" *Endowm*

In the AL
in a paper issu
Members of C
ing passage.

brought to life a romantic fairyland, just as he loved theater for its capacity to give life and reality to more noble poetic conceptions.

Christ Church responsibilities

The blossoming of these interests during his twenties did not lead Dodgson to neglect his study of mathematics and logic. He prepared lectures and courses with earnest care. Christ Church undergraduates often arrived at university totally unacquainted with mathematics and not much interested. Dodgson voiced the age-old teacher's lament of "thankless, uphill work, goading unwilling men to [a] learning they have no taste for, to the inevitable neglect of others who really want to get on." Therefore, his earliest mathematics writings were worksheets and study guides designed for novice students. In 1860 he published his first mathematical works: a *Syllabus of Plane Algebraical Geometry* and *Notes on the First Two Books of Euclid.* The following year *Notes on the First Part of Algebra* and *The Formulae of Plane Trigonometry* appeared.

Dodgson made his debut as the gadfly of Christ Church in 1861. Under review in one of the governing bodies of the college was a proposal to increase the endowment of a professorship held by the Greek scholar Benjamin Jowett. The debate one day became rather involved, as academic squabbles easily may, and Dodgson the logician, exasperated, came to his feet for the first time, to ask that the discussion proceed in a more sensible fashion. A shy man, he seems not to have

Samuel Wilberforce, Bishop of Oxford, photographed by Dodgson.

t of the Greek Professorship."

RNATIVE AMENDMENTS recently proposed under the above heading, the attention of ocation is respectfully invited to the follow-

enjoyed the experience much; recording the incident in his diary later, he made a memorandum never again to say more than he had intended before rising. However, despite this momentary impulse toward prudent reserve, he was a born critic. On 22 November he printed the first of many pamphlets satirizing the college administration, this one entitled *Endowment of the Greek Professorship*. Dodgson the pamphleteer was born.

It was expected at this time that he would, as holder of a Christ Church Studentship, enter holy orders. He had been preparing for this step and in 1861 the time came for him to take it. Yet he hesitated. He discussed his obligations with Samuel Wilberforce, the Anglican Bishop of Oxford, and with his friend and colleague Henry Liddon, and made inquiries as to whether his studentship required him to become a priest. In December he did proceed to ordination as a deacon, but there he stopped.

There has been much speculation about why Dodgson, the devout scion of a clerical family, remained merely a deacon. His decision has been variously attributed to his devotion to the theater, a venue still considered disreputable for the clergy; to his stammer, a handicap in the pulpit; and to the academic life, which he was loathe to give up. No doubt these issues all weighed with him as he considered what course to take, but the real sticking point, as so often for him, lay in the abstract realm of principles.

Dodgson could only make a decision of such gravity by examining its deepest meanings. To represent the church and serve as mediator between human beings and God was a profound matter. He found that he could not on his oath say that he truly believed every one of the Church of England's Thirty-nine Articles, and could not approve of—and therefore honestly represent—all the church's positions. And because he could not see in himself every

CLERICAL ELOCUTION LE

BISHOP PUNCH.—" *Now, Sir, let me hear you publish Banns of Marriage.*"
SWELL CANDIDATE FOR ORDERS.—" *I—aw—publ'sh Bannth of Mawidge 'twee*
BISHOP.—" *Stop, Sir, stop. That will never do for us. You had better take*

quality he would want in a clergyman he felt unable to assume this mantle. In the following decade, his sense that he was woefully inferior to his ideal of a spiritual leader caused him to regret with anguish that he had become even a deacon.

A steady life

No one remains exactly the same person throughout a lifetime, but Charles Dodgson was remarkably consistent. Certainly his views developed and matured, and his concerns shifted focus, but between the time he entered university and his thirtieth birthday he had established the interests and habits that were to shape and define him for life. He became an industrious teacher and scholar of mathematics. He was a serious, conscientious, and thoughtful minor clergyman. He loved photography, quickly developed skill and ease with the process, and soon had enough artistic success to exhibit, to review, and to attract famous subjects. Under his pseudonym of Lewis Carroll, he began to publish poetry and prose.

By the time he turned 30, he had established the first of his great friendships with children. Dodgson and the young Liddells called constantly on each other. From this point forward, being a friend, photographer, and entertainer of girls and boys was his favorite recreation and a most seriously held responsibility. One of these girls, Alice Liddell, was about to inspire him to become an author of rare genius as well.

d Woberth, Batchla, and——"
a the commercial line."

Above: Dodgson's haunting portrait of Alice Liddell as a beggar-child, probably from the late 1850s, is his most famous photograph. Enamored of the theater, he enjoyed having his models dress in costumes.

Opposite: this 1861 John Tenniel cartoon from *Punch* magazine about poor enunciation and affected speech among the clergy followed the Bishop of London's decree that he would ordain no candidate who could not read the services properly. Dodgson was sensitive about his own stammer.

"Alice was beginning to get very tired of sitting by her sister on the bank, and of having nothing to do: once or twice she had peeped into the book her sister was reading, but it had no pictures or conversations in it, 'and what is the use of a book,' thought Alice, 'without pictures or conversations?' "

Alice's Adventures in Wonderland,
1865

CHAPTER 3
ALICE IN WONDERLAND

Left: *Carnation, Lily, Lily, Rose*—childhood as a magical garden of marvels and delights, conjured up by the Victorian painter John Singer Sargent. Right: John Tenniel's Alice peers at the tiny door that leads into Wonderland.

Pictures and picnics

The diaries from Charles Dodgson's late twenties are missing; for information on this crucial period of his life, when he was beginning to create his Wonderland, we must rely on letters, the memoirs of his friends, and other documents.

Photography was only one element in his charmed friendship with the Liddell children. Dodgson escorted them to the wondrous University Museum, an airy metal-and-glass confection where he was able to teach in his favorite way, seizing a moment to build naturally on a student's interest and push her thinking a little

Above: the old British Museum in 1845. Museums were places of wonder and whimsy to a Victorian child. Left: a stuffed dodo. This peculiar, long-extinct bird seems made to order for Wonderland.

further. The museum contained a wealth of natural-history specimens from around the world, including a preserved dodo, a large, clumsy, flightless, extinct bird from the African island of Mauritius. Other outings might be to the Magdalen College deer park or the Botanic Gardens—Oxford was full of fascinating people and intriguing odd corners, populated by Gothic gargoyles.

A great treat was to walk through the town to Folly Bridge and rent a boat to row up or down the River Isis (the local name for the stretch of the Thames that flows through Oxford). Alice recalled in a 1932 interview that "when we went on the river...with Mr. Dodgson...he always brought out with him a large basket full of cakes, and a kettle.... On rarer occasions we went out for the whole day with him, and then we took a larger basket with luncheon—cold chicken and

Left: Alice photo-graphed by Dodgson. In later life Alice described a typical photo session: "We used to sit on the big sofa on each side of him, while he told us stories, illustrating them by pencil or ink drawings as he went along. When we were thoroughly happy and amused at his stories, he used to pose us, and expose the plates before the right mood had passed.... Being photographed was...a joy to us and not a penance as it is to most children. We looked forward to the happy hours in the mathematical tutor's rooms."

Nuneham Bridge in the mid-1800s.

salad and all sorts of good things. One of our favorite whole-day excursions was to row down to Nuneham and picnic in the woods there." The estate of Nuneham was five miles downstream from Oxford; its owner, William Harcourt, had built picnic huts and welcomed visitors on Tuesdays and Thursdays.

It was on a Tuesday in June 1862 that Dodgson assembled quite a party to picnic at Nuneham. Along with his sisters Fanny and

*L*eft: this unique 1862 watercolor of three little girls on a riverbank seems to have been painted by Dodgson on or following one of many such picnics with the Liddells. Below: Alice and creatures dry out after emerging from the pool of tears. The members of the river outing to Nuneham found themselves cast as a variety of strange creatures in the tale. In the first version of the story Alice remarks that she, the Lory, and the Eaglet (both are kinds of birds) are just like sisters, that the Duck sang nicely as they came through the water, and that the Dodo fortunately knew the way to a cottage where they dried off.

Elizabeth and their Aunt Lucy, who were visiting at the time, the group included three of the Liddell sisters and Dodgson's friend Robinson Duckworth, a fellow of Trinity College. After spending the afternoon walking in the park, they were drenched on the return trip in a sudden rainstorm. The party walked three miles in the downpour to take shelter in a house, where the gentlemen left the ladies to dry off, walking on and sending transportation back to fetch them. The adventure ended with evening tea in Dodgson's rooms.

Dodgson's room on the Great Quadrangle, commonly known as Tom Quad, at the time when he was writing *Alice in Wonderland.*

Left: Alice with the Dodo, whose name sounded like Do-do-dodgson's when he stammered.

This damp outing would long have been forgotten but for its later transformation in *Alice in Wonderland* into a wetting for another Alice in a pool of her own tears. In the tale the party was transmuted into a congregation of birds: Lorina became the Lory, Edith the Eaglet, Duckworth the Duck, and in a wry reference to his stammer and perhaps to a sense of his own anachronism, Dodgson turned himself into the Dodo.

ALICE

All in the golden afternoon

The friends planned another trip to Nuneham on 3 July 1862, but rain prevented them from going. The next day the estate was not open to the public, so Dodgson, Duckworth, and the girls rowed upriver to the meadow at Godstow and had tea there. Inevitably the children demanded one of Mr. Dodgson's marvelous stories. Duckworth later recalled: "I rowed *stroke* and he rowed *bow* in the famous Long Vacation voyage to Godstow, when the three Miss Liddells were our passengers, and the [*Alice*] story was actually composed and spoken *over my shoulder* for the benefit of Alice Liddell, who was acting as 'cox' of our gig. I remember turning round and saying, 'Dodgson, is this an extempore romance of yours?' And he replied, 'Yes, I'm inventing as we go along.' "

This dreamy afternoon, when Dodgson sent his "heroine straight down a rabbit-

Left: a decorative capital from a 1922 edition of *Alice*. In search of "a new line of fairy-lore," Dodgson impulsively sent Alice tumbling down a rabbit-hole, hoping to dream up novel adventures under the ground.

hole, to begin with, without the least idea what was to happen afterwards" (as he later put it), is described in the official weather records as cool and rainy, but those involved remembered it as a blazingly sunny day, with a heat haze shimmering over the meadow at Godstow. In reality or in the glow of memory it truly was the golden afternoon that Dodgson conjures up in the introductory poem to *Alice in Wonderland*. The warmth of the sun, the gentle rocking of the boat, the murmur of the river, the rapt listeners together stimulated that great mind to an unparalleled flood of mingled logic and whimsy.

In a reminiscence published years later, Alice said that the stories he told that afternoon must have been even better than usual,

since she remembered the trip so well, and because she begged Mr. Dodgson to write the tale down for her. Perhaps it just seemed better, being the adventures of an extraordinary girl named Alice, whereas the stories from other days, according to Dodgson, had "lived and died, like summer midges." Dodgson and Duckworth confirm that it was indeed Alice's pleading that led the storyteller to write down this one tale. He set to work on it the next day.

Dodgson, Duckworth, and the three girls set forth on their momentous outing.

The friendship and the story grew in unison. In August Dodgson noted in his diary another trip to Godstow with the Liddell girls during which he had had to continue the "interminable fairy-tale of *Alice's Adventures*." In March 1863 his diary records that he borrowed a book of natural history from the Deanery to help him with his illustrations for his fable, which at this stage was called *Alice's Adventures Under Ground*. That month he began a poem about Alice, which

We lived beneath the mat
Warm and snug and fat
But one woe, & that
Was the cat!
To our joys
a clog, In
our eyes a
fog, On our
hearts a log
Was the dog!
When the
Cat's away,
Then
the mice
will

The Mouse's Tale was completely rewritten between *Alice's Adventures under Ground* (seen here, in Dodgson's hand-

eventually became the haunting verse that begins "A boat, beneath a sunny sky," and appears at the end of *Through the Looking-Glass*. Merry outings and visits continued regularly.

In a May 1863 diary entry Dodgson remarks, "Heard from

writing) and *Alice in Wonderland*, where it was set in type.

Above: Charles Dodgson with the children of the author George MacDonald.

Mrs. MacDonald about *Alice's Adventures under Ground,* which I had lent them to read, and which they wish me to publish."

He had first met the fantasy novelist George MacDonald, author of *At the Back of the North Wind,* four years earlier, when both were seeing Dr. James Hunt for treatment of their stammers. They became great friends, and soon Dodgson came to know the MacDonald children as well. He chanced upon them in the London sculpture studio of Alexander Munro, where 6-year-old Greville was posing for a statue. He later recounted many adventures with Uncle Dodgson. He and his sister were apparently the first children other than the Liddells to hear *Alice's Adventures under Ground,* and he wrote, "I remember that first reading well, and also my braggart avowal that I wished there were sixty thousand volumes of it!"

The story

Alice's Adventures in Wonderland is a picaresque fantasy concerning a

Above left: Greville N. MacDonald photographed by Dodgson, 1863. When they first met, at a sculptor's studio, Dodgson tried to persuade the boy that he should take the opportunity to have his head exchanged for a marble one. Greville rejected the idea on the grounds that a marble head couldn't speak. Above right: this 1863 Dodgson photograph of Greville's sister Irene with her hair loose is entitled "It won't come smooth."

Left: Dodgson photographed George MacDonald and another daughter, Lily, on 14 October 1863.

7-year-old girl who, "burning with curiosity," follows a White Rabbit with a pocket watch down a hole into an underground world. The story is characterized by sudden, dreamlike shifts of place and time and unexpected transformations and by a pervasive sense of inverted logic. Splendid satiric rhymes and marvelous word play abound. No synopsis of the disjointed plot can capture the book's air of ingenious absurdity, its high whimsy and charm, or the brilliance of its character sketches. The wild unreality of the tale only underscores a satisfying sense of familiarity: have we not all had odd and absurd encounters with peculiar people, or found ourselves in circumstances in which nothing seemed to go as planned?

In Wonderland Alice encounters many

Curiouser and curiouser! Alice shrinks when she drinks from a little bottle and grows larger when she eats a little cake. Three illustrators interpret Alice "opening out like the largest telescope that ever was," near left, right, and opposite: Dodgson's original drawing, a German Alice by Wiltraud Jasper, and Tenniel's color illustration for *The Nursery Alice.*

Above left: a 1980 French illustration of the White Rabbit by Rico Lins. Left: detail of a 1908 illustration by Harry Rountree, who envisioned a whimsical world. Here we see some of its creatures outside the White Rabbit's house.

humorous and eccentric creatures—most of them very opinionated. The White Rabbit sends her on an errand to his house, where she changes size, gets stuck inside, and scuffles with a lizard named Bill. A haughty Caterpillar offhandedly teaches her how to control her dimensions by eating pieces of mushroom.

She becomes entangled in a series of odd, comical situations in which she is generally more reasonable and sensible than everyone else. Her goal

The artist George Soper introduces Alice to an unusual-looking Caterpillar.

Though Tenniel's illustrations are famous, many other talented artists have interpreted the characters of Wonderland. Clockwise from left: the Frog-Footman and Fish-Footman in an American illustration; an Italian Mad Tea-party; a French Cheshire Cat disappears in stages.

is always to find and enter a beautiful garden, though she is often diverted. She comes across a small house where she overhears a Fish-Footman present to a Frog-Footman an invitation from the Queen to the Duchess to attend a

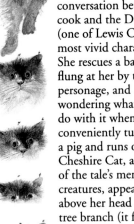

croquet game. In the house she meets a scene of flying dishes, clouds of pepper, and a casually threatening conversation between a cook and the Duchess (one of Lewis Carroll's most vivid characters). She rescues a baby flung at her by this personage, and is wondering what to do with it when it conveniently turns into a pig and runs off. The Cheshire Cat, another of the tale's memorable creatures, appears above her head on a tree branch (it fades in

and out several times in the course of the story) and tries to convince her by logical argument that both she and it are mad. Alice is not persuaded, and proceeds to the home of the March Hare, where she finds

PHIBETAKAPPA
PHIBETAKAPPA
PHIBETAKAPPA!

a large table set up outdoors for tea. In this famous scene, Alice joins a tea-party at which all the other guests are lunatics: the March Hare, a Mad Hatter, and a narcoleptic Dormouse. These converse at length, telling riddles, squabbling, and making very little sense.

Tenniel's Alice meets the Cheshire Cat. Above: a Harvard version of the March Hare and Dormouse. Many of Dodgson's contemporaries were sure he was satirizing Christ Church in the book.

After this she at last enters the enticing garden. It turns out to belong to the King and Queen of Hearts, and Alice is invited to join their croquet game. This is played with flamingos for mallets, hedgehogs for balls, and playing-card soldiers, bent double, for the hoops. As the game degenerates into chaos, the Queen introduces her to the Gryphon, who takes her to meet the Mock Turtle. This pair recites nonsense poems for her and explains, in a pun-filled conversation, what school is like under the sea. The sound of a cry interrupts them and calls them to the trial of the Knave of Hearts, who has been indicted for stealing the tarts of nursery-rhyme fame. In a grand finale, all the characters in the story gather for one of literature's most irrational trials, and Alice is called as a witness. In the time-honored transfigurative tradition of dream stories, she recognizes that most of the people are mere playing-cards and wakes suddenly, brushing away falling leaves.

The distracted Hatter flees the trial, teacup in hand.

Dodgson knew how important pictures were to children, and specified what he wanted from Tenniel. In the

Alice meets John Tenniel

By the end of 1863, with the urging of MacDonald, Dodgson had found a publisher for *Alice,* the London firm of Macmillan. He now set about revising and preparing the text. Although the first version of the manuscript was completed in the spring of 1863, the illustrations caused Dodgson considerable anguish. His well-developed artistic taste made his own shortcomings as a draftsman all too obvious to him, so, with publication in mind, he undertook to find a professional illustrator. In early 1864 Tom Taylor, a playwright and editor of the humor magazine *Punch,* introduced him to a *Punch*

scene where Alice meets the Gryphon, his text advises, "If you don't know what a Gryphon is, look at the picture." This is Dodgson's Gryphon; opposite is Tenniel's.

John Tenniel.

cartoonist named John Tenniel. (In September 1864 Dodgson did complete a set of his own illustrations for the manuscript that he had written out for Alice Liddell as a Christmas gift, but these were not published until 1886.)

Tenniel agreed in April to illustrate the book. Unfortunately, little of his voluminous correspondence with Dodgson survives. Dodgson had always exerted control over his illustrators, even in his early work for *The Train.* He was in regular contact with Tenniel, sketching and describing scenes and characters that he could see in his mind but could not draw to his satisfaction.

He also knew what he wanted from his publisher, and since Dodgson was bearing all the expenses of

Overleaf: two of Tenniel's signature illustrations for *Alice:* the White Rabbit as Herald, colored by another artist in the style of Tenniel, and the pack of cards flying at Alice, colored by Tenniel.

publication himself, he was certainly in a position to have the book designed according to his specifications. In his time this was not uncommon: an author might sell a manuscript outright, lease it for a specific period of time, or arrange any number of different contracts to share expenses and profits. Dodgson had first met Alexander Macmillan in 1863 at the home of Thomas Combe, who ran Oxford's Clarendon Press. Macmillan had recently published Charles Kingsley's popular children's book *The Water Babies* and was interested in Dodgson's fairy tale. So Dodgson and Macmillan entered into a commission agreement in which the author would bear the expenses of publishing his book and the

Above left: *A Grotesque Old Woman,* a 1513 Flemish Renaissance painting by Quinten Massys, is the source for Tenniel's Duchess, above right.

Charles Kingsley's *The Water Babies* was an immensely popular Victorian children's book contemporary with the *Alice* books. It too featured magical encounters. This illustration is by Jessie Wilcox Smith.

publisher would receive a small percentage of the gross profits for producing and distributing it. This allowed Dodgson total control over the book, while benefiting from the guidance of an established publishing house. His numerous letters, on large issues and trifling details, were addressed directly to Alexander Macmillan, and the two established a close and lifelong relationship, combining talents to publish the book that Dodgson envisioned. They determined that *Alice's Adventures under Ground* would be five by seven inches, bound in smooth red cloth with gold stamping.

Dodgson now rewrote and expanded the story, removing personal jokes understandable only to his friends. He almost doubled its length, adding such memorable scenes as the Mad Tea-party and Alice's encounter with the Cheshire Cat. The original title, *Alice's Adventures under Ground,* did not seem fitting, and after considering a number of options—would the world today admire *Alice's Hour in Elfland*?—he settled on *Alice's Adventures in Wonderland,* which is commonly shortened to *Alice in Wonderland.* The book appeared in July 1865 and Dodgson immediately dispatched a number of inscribed copies, some specially bound, to friends young and old.

Alice appears, disappears, and reappears

Then came a letter from John Tenniel, dissatisfied with the printing of the pictures. The cause of his complaint is not entirely clear today, but some copies of the original

Harry Rountree's 1928 edition of *Alice* is full of vigorous line drawings. If a real cat could grin, surely this is what it would look like.

edition were too heavily inked, so that the type bled through to the reverse side of the page, marring the pictures. If Tenniel's copy was one of these, his distress was certainly justified. Dodgson consulted with Macmillan and in August they decided to scrap the first set of sheets and start over, improving both printing and typesetting. Conscientious in all things, Dodgson throughout his career insisted upon first-rate production of his books, whatever the cost. His high standards proved expensive, however: a gloomy diary entry on 18 August tots up the accounts, figuring on a loss of £200 if the first 2,000 copies were sold; if a second

2,000 could be sold, the enterprise would break even.

A*lice in Wonderland* had many imitators. Above: *A New Alice in the Old Wonderland* finds that the Cheshire Cat has had kittens. Left: Davy visits Robinson Crusoe on his island in *Davy and the Goblin.*

Three months later a happier diary entry describes the new press pages as "very *far* superior to the old, and in fact a perfect piece of artistic printing." *Alice's Adventures in Wonderland* came before the public at last in November 1865 (dated 1866) and immediately received complimentary reviews that singled it out from the other children's books of that Christmas season. The newspapers commented on its charm and attractiveness ("an antidote to a fit of the blues," wrote *The Reader*), though one dissenting voice, in *The Athenaeum*, found it "stiff" and "over-wrought." The well-known name of John Tenniel attracted notice in the press, and the fledgling classic sold well. Dodgson had earned back his costs the next year, with 10,000 copies printed by 1867, 35,000 by 1872, and 78,000 by 1886.

Children's stories become rare-book legends

As for the first, badly printed books, after considering selling them as waste paper, Dodgson decided instead to sell all 1,950 unbound sets of sheets to an American publisher, D. Appleton. Many of these still exist today and are a collector's item. More significant still are the fifty copies that were bound and sent to the author's friends and family before the edition was recalled. These are the true first edition of one of the most important children's books in the world, and they hold a special place in the annals of rare-book collecting. Dodgson asked the recipients to send them back in exchange for a better copy and donated the inferior ones to children's hospitals and the like. Twenty-two of these are extant

On the several occasions that editions of *Alice* had to be recalled, Dodgson donated the faulty books to children's hospitals. He always had the greatest sympathy for sick

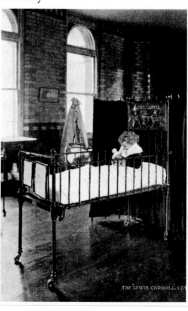

THE LEWIS CARROLL COT

children; fittingly, shortly after his death, children gave their pennies for a bed, the "Lewis Carroll Cot," at the Hospital for Sick Children, Great Ormond Street, London, in his memory.

today. Over the years several have sold at auction for prodigious sums, and all but five have been acquired by museum and library rare-book collections.

What became of Alice's gift?

The original longhand manuscript of *Alice's Adventures under Ground* has had a lively and interesting history as well. Regrettably, Dodgson seems to have destroyed all of his notes and drafts for the book, and does not comment in his diaries on the process of developing the story. Only the final copy itself still exists.

Before reaching its present home at the British Museum, it had some adventures of its own. In 1926 Alice sold it; it was acquired by an American book dealer at Sotheby's auction house in 1928 for the then-record price of £15,400, and was resold in 1946 for $50,000. A group of Americans bought it in 1948 and the Librarian of Congress, Luther Evans, took it to England on the *Queen Elizabeth* and presented it as a gift to the British people, in appreciation for their gallantry in the Second World War.

Estrangement

Walks and outings with the Liddell children had continued frequently and casually into 1863. A large river party to Nuneham in

Chapter 1

Alice was beginning to get very tired of sitting by her sister on the bank, and of having nothing to do: once or twice she had peeped into the book her sister was reading, but it had no pictures or conversations in it, and where is the use of a book, thought Alice, without pictures or conversations? So she was considering in her own mind, (as well as she could, for the hot day made her feel very sleepy and stupid,) whether the pleasure of making a daisy-chain was worth the trouble of getting up and picking the daisies, when a white rabbit with pink eyes ran close by her.

There was nothing very remarkable in that, nor did Alice think it so very much out of the way to hear the rabbit say to itself "dear, dear! I shall be too late!" (when she thought it over afterwards, it occurred to her that she ought to have wondered at this, but at the time it all seemed quite natural); but when the rabbit actually took a watch out of its waistcoat-pocket, looked at it, and then hurried on, Alice started to her feet, for

Two pages from the facsimile edition of Dodgson's original, handwritten gift to Alice, *Alice's Adventures under Ground*. The book itself is on display in London's British Museum.

June of that year included Dodgson and two other gentlemen, the three Liddell sisters, both their parents, and the dean's father. Most of the group came home by carriage, but Dodgson, Lorina, Alice, and Edith returned by railway. His diary records this as a very pleasant conclusion to a pleasant excursion, but the very next page has been cut out with a razor and the Liddell children are not mentioned again until 5 December, when he notes an accidental encounter with them and their mother. He writes: "But I held aloof from them as I have done all this term."

Far left: a modern reproduction of one of the earliest pieces of Alice merchandise. In 1892 the brother of one of Dodgson's friends, a manufacturer of tins, obtained the author's permission to produce the Looking-Glass Biscuit Tin. He obligingly posted several hundred as gifts to Dodgson's friends, young and old. Dodgson did not like the implication that he was endorsing a brand of biscuits, but the tins were very handsome and are now extremely rare.

What had happened to disrupt this unique friendship? The deletion of three days from the diary was made not by Dodgson but by his niece, after his death. In censoring the diary the Dodgson family unwittingly focused the unquenchable curiosity of posterity on the very issue they had wished to obscure.

The "Alice Statue" in Central Park, New York. Since 1958 the Delacorte statue of Alice has been climbed on by countless children.

This rather melodramatic circumstance has encouraged wild speculation about the nature of Dodgson's relationship with Alice and of the quarrel between him and the Liddells. The obvious conclusion is that Dodgson had asked the dean if he might court Alice, then 11 years old, when she came of age, an arrangement not uncommon at the time, but one that would presumably have been unacceptable to the Liddells for social reasons. Charles Dodgson was more than respectable, but the dean's uncle was an earl, and a modest don was not at all what the glamorous Mrs. Liddell had planned for her beautiful daughters. She was known about Oxford as the Kingfisher, eager to marry her children to royalty and nobility. A stammering mathematician from the provinces would never do. Nevertheless, it is plausible to think that Dodgson may have been in love with Alice.

The obvious is not always the correct, however, and there are many other possible explanations for an estrangement. The Liddells may have asked him to keep company less often with the girls as they grew up. A suggestion of ungentlemanly behavior would have been a great insult to him. Dodgson had earlier agreed with the Liddells that Lorina, now 14, was too old to be seen any longer with a gentleman unchaperoned. Nevertheless, he may have been affronted. Dodgson was sensitive, the temper of the times was strict, and the Liddells were ready for the nursery entertainer to fade away and allow the older girls to become young ladies.

Whatever may have occurred, the rupture was not complete. In mid-December Dodgson had dinner at the Deanery and passed a very pleasant evening with the children and Mrs. Liddell. In May he encountered the three older girls and their governess on a walk and chatted with them. This must have given him hope that the old ways might resume, for the following week he records that for several days he had been asking in vain for permission for a river trip. He had invited the three younger girls, Alice, Edith, and Rhoda, "but Mrs. Liddell will not let *any* come in the future—rather superfluous caution." This remark suggests that the Liddells' concern for Lorina's reputation was the cause of the quarrel.

The halcyon days were never to return, and after this the Liddell sisters virtually disappear from Dodgson's diaries. Alice received her handwritten story at the end of 1864, and the published book a year later. In May 1865 Dodgson saw her and the governess in Tom Quad at Christ Church and wrote: "Alice seems changed a good deal, and hardly for the better—probably going through the usual awkward stage of transition." By 1865, when the 13-year-old Alice received her vellum-bound published copy of *Alice's Adventures in Wonderland*, the Golden Afternoon of their friendship had already come to an end.

Strolls in the park, outings, and picnics such as those on which Dodgson accompanied the Liddell sisters were a common pastime in Victorian England.

"You may have great mathematical abilities, but so have hundreds of others. This talent [for fairy tales] is peculiarly your own, and as an Englishman you are almost unique in possessing it. If you covet fame, therefore, it will be (I think) gained by this."

Letter to Dodgson from Mrs. Gatty, editor of *Aunt Judy's Magazine,* 1867

CHAPTER 4

A PRIVATE MAN AND HIS PUBLIC LIFE

Left: Dodgson sought and enjoyed the solid, quiet life of an educated Victorian gentleman. Even the bohemian Pre-Raphaelite artists he admired, such as Dante Gabriel Rossetti (pictured here with a friend) lived comfortably. Right: Tenniel's illustration of the Sheep's mysterious shop in *Through the Looking-Glass* was based on a real shop in Oxford, near the university.

Life and work above ground

While Dodgson put much effort into developing *Alice in Wonderland,* he maintained his other obligations and interests, and wrote on a variety of subjects. In October 1863 he published a pamphlet on Euclid, the father of geometry, and by late 1865 he had begun his treatise on determinants, an algebraic tool. University politics and business seem to have stirred him as much as mathematics. In January 1864 he had a disagreement with the dean concerning the awarding of Studentships, and in March publicly resigned his position as examiner in mathematics because he felt that the new Examination Statute lowered university standards and degraded the degrees offered.

A year later he was among a group of Christ Church Students who demanded more influence in academic administration, and wrote a comic squib on the issue, titled *American Telegrams.* This was circulated through the college, giving news of the proceedings in the form of sham Civil War bulletins. The following month Dodgson commented on another university matter, the debate over the stipend for Benjamin Jowett's professorship, which was still unresolved, in a witty mock mathematical pamphlet, *The New Method of Evaluation as Applied to* π. Before the year was out, as the first faulty printing of *Alice in Wonderland* was going to press, he issued *Dynamics of a Parti-cle,* satirizing human political behavior in terms of geometric axioms and postulates; the word *Parti-cle* is used as a pun on *political party.*

His career as a poet continued as well, with four contributions in 1862 to *College Rhymes,* a periodical he edited for a time. "Disillusionised" is a comic poem that

THE NEW METHOD
or
EVALUATION,
AS APPLIED TO π.

The problem of evaluating π, which has engaged the attention of mathematicians from the earliest ages, had, down to our own time, been considered as purely arithmetical. It was reserved for this generation to make the discovery that it is really a *dynamical* problem: and the true value of π, which appeared an "ignis fatuus" to our forefathers, has been at last obtained under pressure.

The following are the main data of the problem :—

Let U = the University, G = Greek, and P = Professor. Then GP = Greek Professor; let this be reduced to its lowest terms, and call the result J.

Also let W = the work done, T = the Times, ρ = the given payment, π = the payment according to T, and S = the sum required; that π = S.

The problem is, to obtain a value for π which shall be commensurable with W.

In the early treatises on this subject, the value assigned to π was found to be 40.000000. Later writers suspected that the decimal point had been accidentally shifted, and that the proper value is 400.00000: but, as the details of the process for obtaining it had been lost, no further progress was made in the subject till our own time, though several most ingenious methods were tried for solving the problem.

Of these methods we proceed to give some brief account. The [...] note appear to be Rationalisation, the Method [...] [...]hod, and the Method of Elimination.

Top: the first page of *The New Method of Evaluation as Applied to* π. Above: Tom Taylor, editor of *Punch,* was a member of Dodgson's literary and theatrical circle and was photographed by him in 1863.

carries to extremes the conventional charms of a poet's sweetheart, while "Stolen Waters" is a melodramatic ballad about the corruption of a young knight by false love.

Through the sculptor Alexander Munro, Dodgson met Tom Taylor, editor of *Punch*. Munro also introduced him to the Rossetti family: Dante Gabriel Rossetti, the Pre-Raphaelite painter, and his sister Christina, a poet, who, he opined, should have succeeded Tennyson as Poet Laureate. Through the painter Holman Hunt he met another Pre-Raphaelite, John Everett Millais. He had begun to move with ease in the most interesting artistic and literary circles of London.

"The one I have always most wished to meet"

Dodgson had long been an admirer of the celebrated Terry family of actors and met some of them

through Tom Taylor in the summer of 1864. In December he met Kate and then Ellen Terry, the most talented and famous of the family. He had been enchanted with her since her stage debut in 1856, and now found her "lively and pleasant, almost childish in her fun, but perfectly ladylike."

Dodgson had great admiration for all the members of the talented Rossetti family. In the photograph below at left he poses Dante Gabriel Rossetti playing chess with his mother, while Christina and another sister look on. Below: Rossetti's Pre-Raphaelite painting *Golden Water (Princess Parisade).*

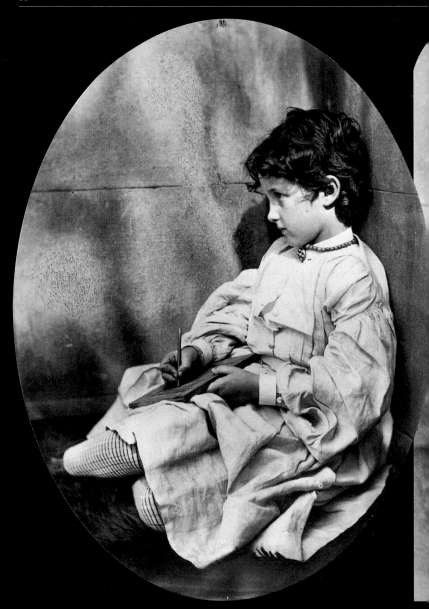

The following July Dodgson spent three white-stone days in London photographing the Terrys, and the last day must especially have delighted him, for he also went to Macmillan's to sign twenty copies of his new book, *Alice in Wonderland*. He then photographed the Terrys for three hours and played Castle Croquet, a game of his own invention, with Kate, Ellen, and Polly, one of the children and always a special friend of his. He finished the day by escorting Polly to the theater on Kate's season ticket. This is the sort of day that Charles Dodgson cherished.

Morning Clouds

The fifteen years after the publication of *Alice* saw his most varied and public activity, and a good deal of writing. While we may regret that many Lewis Carroll stories perished unpublished, it was no one's loss that the next major project he conceived was never realized. In January 1866 he wrote a melodrama entitled *Morning Clouds,* about a boy who is kidnapped by his scheming uncle and eventually restored to his widowed mother.

Dodgson admired the power of drama to stir the soul, and he longed to have that effect on an audience. But his efforts were painfully amateur and he discovered that a gift for literature does not necessarily translate well to the stage. Another master of language, his contemporary Henry James, was equally stagestruck and also wrote a play; like Dodgson, he was unable to transcend melodrama, to cross the line from emotional manipulation to art. Dodgson's closing scene was a tableau in which the reunited family is gathered in the firelight, the children singing their grandfather to sleep. He keenly felt the beauty of this moment, which in its static lyricism comes from the mind of a photographer, not a dramatist.

Publishing and parodies

As a mathematician Dodgson was not in the forefront of the field, but his work was sound, original, and thoughtful. He was interested in designing a new,

AN

ELEMENTARY TREATISE

ON

DETERMINANTS

WITH THEIR APPLICATION TO

SIMULTANEOUS LINEAR EQUATIONS AND ALGEBRAICAL GEOMETRY.

BY

CHARLES L. DODGSON, M.A.

STUDENT AND MATHEMATICAL LECTURER OF CHRIST CHURCH, OXFORD.

Lewis Carroll.

London:
MACMILLAN AND CO.
1867.

The title page of Dodgson's *Elementary Treatise on Determinants,* which included his condensation method for finding the value of determinants. His paper on that subject was presented to the Royal Society in 1866.

Previous pages: the painter Millais's daughters Effie, left, and Mary, right, photographed by Dodgson in 1865.

streamlined way of using algebraic determinants and in 1867 published *An Elementary Treatise on Determinants,* not a pamphlet or study guide, but his first book for the mathematics community. It sold slowly but steadily, and its concepts were innovative and elegant. An apocryphal anecdote circulated, and is still sometimes printed as true, that Queen Victoria was so charmed by *Alice in Wonderland* that she asked the author to send her his next book, and so he duly posted off *An Elementary Treatise.* Dodgson was not amused; a conservative man, he respected his sovereign and refuted the tale in a note appended to *Symbolic Logic.*

Meanwhile, within Oxford, the question of university reform continued to provide an endless stream of controversies. Dodgson's conservative leanings and scorn for illogical thinking kept his pen dipped in parody. Throughout the 1860s his pamphlets appeared. In *The Offer of the Clarendon Trustees,* a witty parody of a request by the natural-sciences department for special facilities, Dodgson applied the same thinking to the needs of the mathematics department, demanding a "room for reducing Fractions to their Lowest Terms. This should be provided with a cellar for keeping the Lowest Terms when found…[and a] narrow strip of ground, railed off and carefully leveled for…testing practically whether Parallel Lines meet or not: for this purpose it should reach, to use the expressive language of Euclid, 'ere so far.' "

Dodgson's portrait of his friend Henry Parry Liddon.

Russia: Orthodoxy and art

Dodgson left the British Isles only once, traveling for two months to Germany and Russia in 1867 with his friend and fellow cleric Henry Liddon. Their voyage brought them face to face with the Eastern church. Dodgson and Liddon, devout Anglicans, were both profoundly engaged in a debate, widespread in Britain, between High Church and Low Church practices, between sympathy for the rich ceremony of Catholicism and Eastern Orthodoxy and sympathy for the austerity of Evangelical Christianity. For practicing English Protestants these issues were urgent, much discussed, and often divisive.

William Morris's medieval-revival textiles (left) were immensely popular in Victorian Britain. Below: James McNeill Whistler's *Blue and Gold: The Rose Azalea,* c. 1890–95, was influenced by Japanese art. Morris and Whistler represented new aesthetic trends in England; both were well-known in Oxford, where their art styles were much debated. Dodgson preferred the more conservative Pre-Raphaelites.

Dodgson was far from insensitive to the role of aesthetics in religion. Indeed, a need to apprehend the spiritual through art was a hallmark of his character. He objected not to the beauty of Orthodox services, but to the danger of allowing an emotionally satisfying ritual to become an end itself, rather than a means of access to God. What he loved most about theater, painting, and music was their capacity to communicate spiritual and emotional realities, to convey a higher truth straight to the soul, bypassing the intellect. This desire to find God though art was in a sense a contradictory instinct in him, since he also devoted much effort to constructing logical religious arguments. He had resisted taking priest's orders in part out of a fear that he would be unable to argue convincingly against the sophistry and skepticism with which he would be challenged. His spiritual need

for art encouraged a degree of romantic bad taste. This was the era that produced the aesthetic theories of John Ruskin, Matthew Arnold, and William Morris; the sentimental, moralizing paintings and plays Dodgson admired were about to be swept away by "art for art's sake"—the works of such innovators as James McNeill Whistler and Bernard Shaw. In fact, Whistler, who considered the Pre-Raphaelites vulgar and meretricious, was an almost exact contemporary of Dodgson.

The journey gave Dodgson an opportunity to immerse himself in art, culture, religion, and cultivated debate, though not every encounter with art was transcendent. He made great fun of mannered Prussian statuary: "The two principles of Berlin Architecture appear to me to be these. On the housetops, wherever there is a convenient place, put up the figure of a man; he is best placed standing on one leg. Wherever there is room on the ground, put either a circular group of busts on pedestals, in consultation, all looking inward—or else the colossal figure of a man killing, about to kill, or having killed (the present tense is preferred) a beast."

Throughout his life religion remained an important and difficult issue for Dodgson. His father, like Liddon, was a High Church Anglican, a member of that branch of the Church of England whose traditions remained closer to those of the Catholic church. The debates about Protestant church doctrine were especially pressing at Oxford, still a religious institution. The younger Dodgson, whose religious sense was warmhearted and temperate, was at odds with his father's perspective and could be equally rigorous and uncompromising. Father and son held irreconcilable views on such questions as the morality of attending the theater, and this chasm caused great distress to a dutiful son. In the summer of 1868 Archdeacon Dodgson died suddenly. Dodgson always described the death of this

Archdeacon Dodgson in his later years.

powerful figure as the greatest loss of his life, despite their conflicts.

New homes

Returning to Christ Church in the fall of 1867, Dodgson took up residence in a new, large set of rooms. After his father's death, the next year his family left the rectory in Croft and Dodgson resettled his siblings—none had yet married—and their Aunt Lucy in Guildford, a pleasant town convenient to London and Oxford. He leased a house called The Chestnuts, where the comings and goings of siblings, nephews, and nieces revolved around the hub of the six unmarried sisters. It remained the family head-quarters until 1919.

Through the Looking-Glass

Throughout the later 1860s Dodgson nurtured another project—the continuing adventures of Alice under the working title of *Looking-Glass House.* Notes about a further book in his 1867 and 1869 diaries refer mainly to his efforts to secure an illustrator, well before the text was complete. John Tenniel was willing, but engaged with other projects; Dodgson approached Sir Joseph Noël Paton, whose painting *The Reconciliation of Oberon and Titania* with 165 fairies had so enchanted him ten years earlier, but Paton was ill.

Nineteenth-century piano music based on *Through the Looking-Glass.*

The sitting room of the suite on Tom Quad in Oxford, overlooking St. Aldate's Street, that Dodgson occupied from 1868 until his death. His Arthur Hughes painting, *The Lady with the Lilacs,* is visible on the right. He had a darkroom here and four years later obtained permission to build a glass house, no longer extant, on top of the building, which enabled him to take photographs in studio conditions with strong light.

Dodgson wrote Tenniel, offering to buy his time from his publishers; Tenniel agreed to illustrate the book in his spare time.

The title had evolved to *Behind the Looking-Glass*, but eventually Henry Liddon suggested *Through the Looking-Glass,* and the subtitle *And What Alice Found There* was added. With the splendid Tenniel once more secured, Dodgson set to work in earnest. Unlike *Alice in Wonderland,* a single story told to a particular child, *Looking-Glass* drew together many ideas, stories, and anecdotes from different points in its author's life. The framework of a living chess game, for example, probably makes use of little jokes and incidents from the days when Dodgson was teaching the Liddell children to play chess, before *Alice in Wonderland* was published. The ideas based on mirror reversal—walking away from something in order to go toward it; the White Queen's backward memory—are less organized, and seem to arise from Dodgson's general love of logical inversions.

Part of the text of *Looking-Glass* was delivered to Macmillan's in 1869, but Tenniel was still working on the pictures through 1870. Dodgson tinkered with the story, removing an entire incident, called "The Wasp in a Wig," at Tenniel's suggestion, and finally mailed off the completed manuscript in January 1871. Many details remained to be resolved. Dodgson felt the frontispiece drawing of the Jabberwock was too frightening, and sent

The Jabberwock, "with eyes of flame, came whiffling through the tulgey wood, and burbled as it came!" Dodgson was afraid Tenniel's beast (left) would frighten children. Above: a detail from a Rembrandt etching of *Adam and Eve* suggests that the Edenic serpent—frightening not only to children—may be an ancestor of the Jabberwock.

copies of it to about thirty mothers, to canvass their opinions. He finally decided to place the fearsome Jabberwock within the book, and to use Alice and the White Knight for the frontispiece. The Knight is generally considered to represent Dodgson; he is the gentle, melancholy fabulist ("It's my own invention"), the protector who escorts the young girl through the woods of youth to the threshold of adulthood, striking a note of elegiac resonance.

The book went on sale at Christmas 1871 and by Dodgson's birthday in January had sold 15,000 copies. Perhaps because of film and stage adaptations of *Alice's Adventures in Wonderland* and *Through the Looking-Glass*, the two tales have merged in many readers' minds. Both are filled with marvelous nonsense rhymes and

The High Oxford . . . from M . . .

THROUGH TH

AND WHAT A

Dodgson developed a close association with Oxford High School over the years. Above: his inscription in a gift copy of the second *Alice* book. Left: Alice crosses into Looking-Glass Land. " 'Why, it's turning into a sort of mist now, I declare! It'll be easy enough to get through—' ...And certainly the glass *was* beginning to melt away, just like a bright silvery mist."

unforgettably funny characters. Nevertheless, *Through the Looking-Glass* is a more complex narrative.

The story

Through the Looking-Glass takes place six months after *Alice in Wonderland,* in November. Alice, playing in her family drawing-room, imagines what the room partly visible (reflected) in the mirror might be like and suddenly finds herself able to pass through the glass into it. She finds herself in a room superficially similar to the one she has left, but in which pictures and objects are alive and the writing in books is both backward and fantastical—including the famous nonsense poem "Jabberwocky." She passes into a garden of talking flowers where one has to walk away from things in order to go toward them. This inverted world is also a giant chess board with living players, in which she

In Looking-Glass Land Alice and the Red Queen must run as fast as they can to stay in one place.

is assigned the role of the White Queen's pawn. The rest of the story consists of a real, if peculiar, chess game in which many of Alice's encounters with other people—knights, queens, kings—correspond to chess moves. As in Wonderland, the creatures she meets in Looking-Glass Land are of all sorts, and most are talkative, opinionated, absurd, and given to flights of poetry.

Alice travels by railway. The man in the paper hat is a Tenniel lampoon of Benjamin Disraeli, then the Conservative Party opposition leader, and later prime minister of Great Britain.

Alice makes her first chess move, through the second and third squares, by railway, and then passes through the wood where things have no name. After this, in the fourth square, she meets the first of several nursery-rhyme characters, Tweedledee and Tweedledum, little fat men who echo the book's theme of mirrored pairs, both identical and opposite. Looking-Glass Land, populated with many characters from famous nursery rhymes whose fates are well-known, has more formal structure than the free-form Wonderland.

Alice soon encounters the White Queen and learns

In another illustration in the book, in which the Lion and the Unicorn share a plum-cake with Alice, Tenniel gave the Unicorn Disraeli's face and the Lion that of his great rival, the Liberal prime minister William Gladstone.

more about the oddities of this place where people's memories, like so much else, work backward. In an especially dreamlike transition, this scene melts into a sort of Curiosity Shop (the fifth square), owned by a knitting Sheep. There Alice pursues a fugitive egg into the sixth square, where it turns into Humpty Dumpty, brilliantly imagined as a pompous, opinionated, egg-shaped pedant. After he (inevitably) falls from his wall, all the Kings's horses and all the King's men thunder past, leaving Alice to meet the White King and the Lion and the Unicorn.

She crosses into the seventh square, where the White Knight rescues her from the Red Knight and escorts her to the last square. There she is tested by the Red and White Queens and becomes a queen too. Her celebratory feast grows increasingly bizarre until, as in the first book, she takes control of the scene and ends it, waking from what turns out once again to have been a dream.

These Tweedledee and Tweedledum salt-and-pepper shakers are recent examples of Alice-inspired merchandise.

In the wood with no name Alice and a wild fawn are able to walk together without fear, since neither has an identity.

Other writings

The name Lewis Carroll made other appearances in print during the period when he was developing and preparing *Looking-Glass* for publication. Shortly after his return from Russia, Dodgson's story "Bruno's Revenge" was published in the popular

Humpty Dumpty. Sat on a wall
Humpty Dumpty had a great fall.

The character we know as a large, opinionated egg (above) was not always seen that way. Kate Greenaway, another popular Victorian children's illustrator, saw Humpty Dumpty as a more conventional little boy in 1881 (opposite).

Overleaf, top of page, left: Sylvie and Bruno as they appeared in *Aunt Judy's Magazine* in 1867; and, right, the original illustration by William M'Connell for "Solitude," printed in *The Train,* 1856.

I LOVE the stillness of the wood,
I love the music of the rill,
I love to couch in pensive mood
Upon some silent hill.

children's periodical *Aunt Judy's Magazine*. In this fairy tale, the mischievous fairy Bruno tries to spoil his sister Sylvie's garden, but learns instead a lesson about the joy of doing good for others. This sweet bit of fancy was received with cries for more Bruno stories, but almost two decades were to pass before Sylvie and Bruno reappeared.

Lewis Carroll brought before the public his first book of collected verse in 1869. *Phantasmagoria* contained poems both comic and serious, the majority previously published in periodicals. "Hiawatha's Photographing," "A Sea Dirge," "Stolen Waters," "Solitude," and the Oxford diatribe *The Elections to the Hebdomadal Council* were reprinted. Making its debut, the title poem is a long narrative in which a man discovers that he is being haunted by a small ghost. The phantom explains to him the five rules of haunting—including a maxim that requires lubricating the floor with candle-ends, butter, and suet, in order to glide and swing from side to side—and other tidbits of ghostly life, until they accidentally discover that the ghost has come to the wrong house. The cover design depicts the Crab Nebula, the remnant

of a supernova explosion: cosmic spectacle conveys the concept of the fantastic, or phantasmagoric.

Controversies

Dean Liddell's administrative, political, and ecclesiastic reforms at Christ Church continued to provide opportunities for Dodgson to indulge in humorous and critical essays; in 1874 his *Notes by an Oxford Chiel* [i.e., child] collected several of the Oxford pamphlets in a book. In the mid-1870s he wrote *Some Popular Fallacies about Vivisection,* a critique of the procedure published in the *Fortnightly Review.* While he did not especially dote on animals, he rejected the axiom that humankind has a right to inflict pain on them. He abhorred the brutalizing effect of institutionalized cruelty on those who practice it, expressed fear of the spiritual disaster awaiting those whose sense of mercy is deadened, and raised the specter of a

Above: the ghost from *Phantasmagoria.* Below: Christ Church Cathedral in 1881. Liddell made alterations to the church that Dodgson protested in a pamphlet.

breed of singleminded scientists capable of justifying experimentation on prisoners, lunatics, and anyone perceived to be of lesser worth.

"Here comes Mr. Dodgson!"

Dodgson's social life flourished, with *Alice in Wonderland* now bringing him introductions to all sorts of interesting people, as photography had done in the past. He maintained his friendship with the Terrys and made many new child-friends—in Oxford, on the train, through their parents, at the seaside. Ethel and Julia Arnold, nieces of the poet Matthew Arnold, were favorite friends and photographic models; Julia was the future mother of the author Aldous Huxley.

Ethel's anecdote of a meeting between Dodgson and his child-friends conjures up a vivid picture of an encounter: "A number of little girls, bursting with youthful spirits, and all agog for mischief, danced along one of the paths, a staid governess bringing up the rear. Presently one of their number spied a tall black clerical figure in the distance, swinging along toward the group with a characteristic briskness, almost jerkiness, of step.—'Here comes Mr. Dodgson,' she cried. 'Let's make a barrier across the path so that he can't pass.' No sooner said than done—the children joined hands and formed a line across the path; the clerical figure, appreciating the situation, advanced at the double and charged the line with his umbrella. The line broke in confusion, and the next moment four of the little band were clinging to such portions of the black-coated figure as they could seize upon. Two little people, however, hung back, being seized with shyness and a sudden consciousness of their audacity, a sudden awe of this tall, dignified gentleman in black broadcloth and white tie. But in a moment he had shaken off the clinging, laughing children, and before the two little strangers had time to

An early version of Walt Disney's *Alice*. Below: children at the beach, an illustration from *Aunt Judy's Magazine*, 1867.

realize what had happened, they found themselves trotting along either side of him, a hand of each firmly clasped in the strong, kind hands of Lewis Carroll, and chattering away as if they had known him all their lives. Thus began a lifelong friendship between Lewis Carroll and the younger of these two little girls, myself."

"Just the place for a Snark!"

Dodgson spent much time with his family, in addition to visiting child-friends, celebrated public figures, and his Christ Church colleagues. He often vacationed at Guildford and spent holidays in London with various siblings. By 1871 both his sister Mary and his brother Wilfred had married and had children, to the joy of the "sisterhood"— his term for his six unmarried sisters. His beloved Uncle Skeffington died in 1873, but on the whole his family circle remained full.

Another death in the family was the catalyst for one of Dodgson's greatest literary accomplishments, the long poem *The Hunting of the Snark*. In the summer of 1874 his 22-year-old cousin and godson Charlie Wilcox fell ill with tuberculosis and came to live in the

Henry Holiday's original cover for *The Hunting of the Snark*.

The seven Dodgson sisters, photographed by Dodgson. His ability to compose group portraits is considered one of his main photographic achievements.

mild southern climate of Guildford in an effort to improve his health; he died before the year was out. Dodgson came home during the long summer vacation to help look after the invalid. One day, after a long night sitting up with Charlie, Dodgson went for a walk. As he later explained in his 1887 essay "Alice on the Stage," a detached line of verse popped into his head: "For the Snark *was* a Boojum, you see." It stayed with him and he wrote a stanza to go with it. Over the next two years he devised, all out of order, the poem for which that line became the conclusion.

He engaged Henry Holiday to illustrate *The Hunting of the Snark* and the book proceeded in fits and starts—indeed, the stanzas are called "fits," after an ancient Anglo-Saxon term for the divisions of a poem. Published at Easter 1876, *The Hunting of the Snark* is the balladlike tale of an unusual hunting party who set sail to an island in search of a Snark, a mysterious, imaginary animal invented by Dodgson. They overcome many tragicomic dangers only to find that this particular Snark is a terrible subspecies known as a Boojum. The reviews of the poem were mixed, largely reflecting the disappointment of critics who had expected another *Alice in Wonderland*. Yet *The Hunting of the Snark* has its own fascination: it has great humor and a haunting sense of melancholy, and the highly quotable lines are charged with meaning. As Alice had said of "Jabberwocky," "It seems to fill my head with ideas—only I don't know exactly what they are!" Many

An illustration for *The Hunting of the Snark* by Henry Holiday, 1876: the Butcher and the Beaver form a fast friendship over a mathematics lesson. The influential Oxford art critic John Ruskin, as Dodgson noted in his diary on 23 November 1874, held out "no hopes that Holiday would be able to illustrate a book satisfactorily."

theories have been offered to explain the meaning and possible levels of allegory in *The Hunting of the Snark*. Dodgson claimed that he had intended no one hidden meaning, but was happy for others to find whatever they wished in the tale. Its sinister charm and unplumbed depths have won it something of a cult following, and it stands alongside the *Alice* books as further witness to his genius.

"Work claims my wakeful nights, my busy days—"

In middle age Dodgson had the satisfaction of close friendships in the world of the arts and theater and success in his work and hobbies. He could scarcely have worked harder, yet he was no recluse. In order to preserve his privacy he went to ludicrous lengths to avoid the celebrity of being Lewis Carroll; on the other hand, he was well aware of what his pseudonym could do for him and took advantage of it when it suited him.

But Dodgson was at heart a serious man. As he passed through his forties he increasingly saw himself as old and feared that he would die before accomplishing his real work in mathematics and logic. The focus of his life began to turn from pleasures, friends, and new experiences, to work, work, and yet more work.

The *Cutty Snark* in full sail.

Alice's post-publication career as a spokesperson began early. In this rare 19th-century brochure a character purporting to be the real Alice writes a lengthy letter home to her sister Edith about the wonders of Yellowstone National Park. Alice has since promoted innumerable products, from beer to washing machines.

"Friends wonder sometimes at my refusing all social invitations now, and taking no holidays. But when old age has begun, and the remaining years are *certainly* not many, and the work one wishes to do, before the end comes, is *almost* certainly more than there is time for, I think one cares less for so-called 'pass-times.' *I* want the time to go more *slowly,* not more *quickly!*"

Letter to Mrs. Blakemore,
28 October 1889

CHAPTER 5
FROM WONDERLAND TO THE WORLD

Left: another dreamy inventor, the White Knight is generally considered to be Dodgson's representative in Looking-Glass Land. Right: this 15th-century bronze medallion of an Italian Renaissance ruler is probably the source for Tenniel's White Knight (Rembrandt also borrowed the figure, in reverse, for an etching).

A man of letters

As *Alice* began to bring Charles Dodgson a good income he went out of his way to discover and meet the needs of friends and relatives, paying for lessons, holidays, extravagances, and necessities. He made gifts, not loans, and wrote many letters for those in need of patronage for a career or cause. Letter writing, an outgrowth of his rich social life and literary fame, consumed much of his time.

He maintained a vast correspondence with children and adults, which he logged meticulously in a letter register, a typically Dodgsonian device in which was recorded and numbered a *précis* of each letter sent and received. Through this contrivance—a precursor of the database—he could track an exchange over many years. Characteristically, the letter register solves a problem in an exact and complete way that is more complicated and time-consuming than the size of the problem warrants. Like some of his mnemonic devices and his tennis tournament system (completely fair and totally impractical), it is primarily an exercise to delight the lover of processes. The register indicates over 100,000 letters sent and received in Dodgson's lifetime, not including quick notes or messages.

In a book called *Navigation with Alice* the Caterpillar impatiently teaches Alice the concepts of celestial navigation.

Euclid's modern champion

Beginning in 1877, when he was 45 years old, and for the next two decades, he took holiday lodgings at Eastbourne on England's south coast during the summer months. Brothers

A page from Dodgson's 1879 book *Euclid and His Modern Rivals.* Dodgson used a conversational format to make a sensible examination of the facts and fallacies concerning Euclid plain to any reader.

and sisters, nieces and nephews, child-friends and adult friends came to stay there, and Dodgson often traveled to Guildford and London.

The work occupying his mind in the late 1870s was geometry, and in particular a defense of Euclid, published in 1879 as *Euclid and His Modern Rivals.* Other less urgent projects were an illustrated edition of *Phantasmagoria,* eventually known as *Rhyme? and Reason?,* illustrated by Arthur B. Frost, and several word games, notably *Doublets,* published as a small book in 1879. Still seen today, *Doublets* requires the player to link two words, preferably opposite in meaning or humorously connected, with a chain of other words, changing one letter in each word along the chain (e.g., evolve the word MAN from the word APE. Solution: APE–are–ere–err–ear–mar–MAN).

Two pages from *Doublets,* with challenges set by Dodgson.

A fellow traveler in Fairyland

Life at Oxford suited Dodgson; in that congenial milieu of wits, geniuses, and eccentrics he established many warm and longstanding friendships with colleagues. Still, in 1879 he found a soulmate outside the university who filled a need not within Oxford's compass. He had written to an artist whose pictures of fairies he admired, and they struck up a correspondence. E. Gertrude Thomson was 29 when they met at London's Victoria and Albert Museum, then known as the South Kensington Museum. After his death, in an 1898 reminiscence called "Lewis Carroll," she recalled:

Arthur B. Frost's illustration from *Rhyme? and Reason?* of the wild man going his weary way.

A little before twelve I was at the rendezvous, and then the humour of the situation suddenly struck me, that *I* had not the ghost of an idea what *he* was like, nor would *he* have any better chance of discovering *me*!... Just as the big clock had clanged out twelve, I heard the high vivacious voices and laughter of children sounding down the corridor. At that moment a gentleman entered, two little girls clinging to his hands, and as I caught sight of the tall, slim figure, with the clean-shaven, delicate, refined face, I said to myself, "*That's* Lewis Carroll." He stood for a moment, head erect, glancing swiftly over the room, then bending down, whispered something to one of the children; she, after a moment's pause, pointed straight at me. Dropping their hands he came forward, and with that winning smile of his that utterly banished the oppressive sense of the Oxford don, said simply, "I am Mr. Dodgson; I was to meet you, I think?" To which I as frankly smiled and said, "How did you know me so soon?" "My little friend found you. I told her I had come to meet a young lady who knew fairies, and she fixed on you at once. But, I knew you before she spoke."

They became fast friends and often visited the theater and art galleries, looked at photographs, and drew together. Dodgson's joy in the company of little girls remained throughout his life, but his companionship with Thomson offered a glimpse of his later years, when, with his marital intentions no longer at issue, the strict social code of the day permitted him to have "child"-friends in their twenties without raising eyebrows. As he wrote to the mother of one such friend when he was 64, "Child-society is very delightful to me: but I confess that grown-up society is much more interesting!"

Dodgson seems never to have found romantic love, but in Gertrude Thomson he discovered a comfortable adult companion who shared his pleasure in fairy lore and with whom he could develop his largely thwarted dream of drawing.

He makes his time his own

Approaching his fiftieth birthday, Dodgson decided to resign his mathematics lectureship. He had held the post for half his life. Much of his mathematics work had been devoted to making the subject understandable to beginners and amateurs, perhaps at the expense of more advanced studies. He delivered his final lecture on 30 November 1881, expressing the sadness one feels when something important in life comes to an end.

Despite the presence of so many documents revealing the particulars of Charles Dodgson's life, crucial points lie in darkness, inadequately explained: his decision not to take priest's orders; the break with the Liddells and related missing diary pages; and, in 1880, the end of his career as a photographer. Photography was a difficult, time-consuming, and expensive hobby, requiring cumbersome, heavy equipment, which he had already stopped bringing to Eastbourne.

Dodgson lived virtually his entire adult life within Oxford's beautiful walls. The interior of Christ Church Hall has changed little since he ate his meals there, except that his portrait now hangs among the others and one of the stained-glass windows honors him.

He did not seem to know at the time that he had taken his last photograph. After a matter-of-fact reference to a session at the end of the season, he simply did not take it up again. It is hard to know how much significance this turn of events deserves; after all, hobbies do not always last a lifetime. Still, this was an avocation from which he had drawn renown, social connections, and great artistic satisfaction. Its sudden end has seemed mysterious to some biographers, who have conjectured that an unrecorded scandal, perhaps involving nude photography of little girls, forced him to quit. This melodramatic notion is purely speculative, supported by no evidence. While Dodgson would have gone to any lengths to protect the reputations of his young models, to give up nude photography—and not other forms of photography—would have addressed such a scandal

Dodgson sometimes had his prints professionally colored and backgrounds painted in. In this photograph of the sisters Annie and Frances Henderson as shipwrecked Robinson Crusoes the girls' nudity has been somewhat disguised. He always wished to be thought a serious artist; approaching the traditional subject of the nude with child models may have been a way to depict the unclothed human form without sexual overtones.

sufficiently. It is also unlikely that outraged citizens could have forced Dodgson to do anything he did not wish to do. For a few years into the 1880s he indicated his intention to continue photography, and it seems sensible to conclude that the sketching of clothed and nude child models gradually replaced photography as his artistic outlet in the limited time he was willing to devote to such things.

Irons in the fire

After his resignation as a lecturer, Dodgson considered in his diary his plans for a "new form of life." He hoped to do some "worthy work in writing—partly in the cause of Mathematical education, partly in the cause of innocent recreation for children, and partly, I hope…in the cause of religious thought." He listed the books he was contemplating: a revision of *Euclid and His Modern Rivals,* the illustrated edition of *Phantasmagoria,* a collection of puzzles to be done in the head that in 1893 became *Pillow Problems,* further writing on Euclid, a book on squaring the circle, a method of finding logarithms and sines without tables, a book of serious poetry, a book of games and puzzles, and his last work of fiction, the novel *Sylvie and Bruno.* He also planned an expurgated edition of Shakespeare for girls under the age of 18, with all the bawdy double entendres removed, which he never completed.

He seems to have tackled his agenda with relish: his diary entries record much writing, including pamphlets and letters to the editor of *The St. James's Gazette* on voting methods. This was a topic he was to study in depth, as it involved two things close to his heart—mathematical theorizing and scrupulous fairness in matters of social and political importance.

In 1885 his list of literary "irons in the fire" also comprised more work on Euclid, a book on symbolic logic, the puzzle book *A Tangled Tale,* and two *Alice* projects. Dodgson first suggested *The Nursery Alice* to Macmillan in 1881. This was a picture book for very young children. When the book came out in 1889 it suffered as the first edition of *Alice in Wonderland* had from faulty printing. In this case, when Dodgson saw the printed sheets he thought them gaudy to the point of vulgarity and ordered a new printing with better color reproduction. The rejected first set of pages was shipped to America; Dodgson assumed that the garish colors would appeal to American tastes. In fact the American publisher did not think them colorful enough.

The cover illustration for *The Nursery Alice* was by Gertrude Thomson; inside, Tenniel colored some of his earlier *Alice* illustrations.

Opposite: Thomson's 1898 illustration of fairies for Dodgson's posthumous work *Three Sunsets* typifies the idealized nude-child-as-fairy that sentimental Victorians favored on greeting cards and the like.

Dodgson now also wrote to Alice Hargreaves, asking permission to publish in facsimile the manuscript book that he had given her years earlier as a Christmas gift. Given the success of *Alice in Wonderland* he thought the public might like to see its earlier incarnation.

Alice lent him the book to be photographed for the edition, which was published in 1886. Simultaneously, he published *The Game of Logic,* a sudden inspiration that was executed without even appearing on his list of writing projects. This was both a game and a teaching device that used counters and a

The Game of Logic book cover, board, and counters. This was both a game and a teaching device, used to demonstrate how a syllogism works.

A passage from *Curiosa Mathematica II:*

18. (21, 41)

Find a Point, in the base of a given Triangle, such th
if from it perpendiculars be dropped upon the sides,
line joining their extremities shall be parallel to the ba
(1) Trigonometrically. (2) Geometrically. [11

board to demonstrate the mechanisms of a logical progression.

Nine years in a curatorship

Oddly, having freed himself from many college responsibilities, in 1882 Dodgson became curator of the Christ Church Common Room, a sort of club-cum-meeting room. Inevitably, something that absorbed his attention was bound to find its way into printed form. In 1884 he published *Twelve Months in a Curatorship by One Who Has Tried It,* followed by *Three Years in a Curatorship by One Whom It Has Tried,* in 1886. These pamphlets report wryly on the state of the Common Room and the tribulations of its curator. He observes— only half-facetiously—in the preface to the latter: "Long

Pillow Problems, showing the sort of problems Dodgson offered as a mental occupation when lying awake in the dark. *Pillow Problems* was meant to provide distractions for the troubled and sleepless mind; it caused Dodgson's friends some concern about his health.

and painful experience has taught me one great principle in managing business for other people, *viz.*, if you want to inspire confidence, *give plenty of statistics.…* A curator who contents himself with simply *doing* the business…is sure to be distrusted.… But, only circulate some abstruse tables of figures, particularly if printed in lines and columns, so that ordinary readers can make nothing of them, and…[then they cry:] 'We trust you entirely!' "

Ellen Terry

The 1880s were a grand time in the English stage, whose reigning monarchs were the actors Ellen Terry and Henry Irving and the operettists William Gilbert and Arthur Sullivan. Dodgson adored them all. His long friendship with Terry saw some rough patches: he had ceased social contact with her in 1868 when she went to live, unmarried, with the architect Edwin Godwin. Dodgson had deep sympathy for Terry, who had left a loveless marriage to the painter George Frederic Watts (who in turn was mentor to Dodgson's fellow photographer Julia Margaret Cameron). He did not consider that she had violated the laws of God, since Watts had broken their contract first, and he saw no spiritual fault in her living with Godwin. But as a strict Victorian gentleman he found it impossible to associate with her until 1877, when she remarried:

Above: a detail from James McNeill Whistler's portrait of Sir Henry Irving in his costume for Tennyson's play *Queen Mary*. Irving was the leading actor of his day, especially noted for his performances in Shakespeare and Tennyson works. Left: Ellen Terry was often Irving's leading lady; she acted opposite him as Portia (seen here) in *The Merchant of Venice* in 1875. This portrait was printed on postcards, to be collected by fans. A good friend, Terry often invited Dodgson and his young theater guests backstage and occasionally acted as patron to aspiring actresses whom he was championing.

privately he could appreciate her situation, but he could not endorse it publicly. Whether Terry understood or simply forgave his limitations, she showed herself to be gracious and large-hearted, and resumed a merry friendship with him. He had the ear of the greatest actress of his time; she had the devotion of Lewis Carroll.

Writing for the theater

The possibility of staging *Alice in Wonderland* had occurred to Dodgson early on, and in his diaries he mentions some of his ideas and initial attempts to sketch out a dramatic version. Over the years he

negotiated with Mr. and Mrs. German Reed, producers of respectable family entertainments, and approached the composer Sullivan (partner of Gilbert) to have him set some of the songs to music. Sadly, nothing came of this beguiling idea.

In 1886 he found a good collaborator in the playwright Henry Savile Clarke, who approached him, wishing to create an operetta from *Alice in Wonderland* and *Through the Looking-Glass*. Dodgson stipulated that there be no hint of coarseness in the production—an edict prompted by the vulgar jokes for adults that often peppered children's plays of the era. During four months of development he made a great many more suggestions, some of which Clarke used. For the role of Alice Dodgson proposed Phoebe Carlo, a child actress and friend. Clarke agreed to cast her, but objected to Dodgson's wish to design her costumes. Dodgson responded graciously, writing to Clarke: "I will now execute that beautiful strategic movement known as 'giving way all along the line' & withdraw my suggestions 'en masse,' the 'dress' question included—Amateurs have no business to put in their oar: it only spoils things."

Alice has been set to music more than once. Above: this 1950 phonograph record is one of many recordings, tapes, and compact disks telling the story, in English and other languages. Some have celebrity readers and singers. Left: the playwright and impresario Henry Savile Clarke interpreted *Alice* in an operetta. Dodgson always desired to realize the book as a play, but he lacked confidence in his ability to oversee a production of sufficiently high quality, and the project was long in the making.

Alice in Wonderland, a Dream Play for Children, opened at the Prince of Wales's Theatre in London on 23 December 1886, the day after the facsimile edition of *Alice's Adventures under Ground* was published ("A tolerably eventful week for me!" reads the diary entry). With music by Walter Slaughter, libretto by Clarke, and some revisions by Dodgson, the operetta successfully brought the familiar stories to the stage, and earned good reviews and enthusiastic audiences. Dodgson derived great satisfaction from observing incognito the public enjoying his work. In a letter to a friend, he wrote: "We had a chatty old gentleman next to us, who told us, 'The author of *Alice* has written a letter to that little girl that plays the part, and has given her a book. And she has written to tell

The program from the original production of Clarke's 1886 operetta.

Phoebe Carlo as Alice, with Dorothy D'Alcourt as the Dormouse.

him she will do her very best.' 'Indeed!' I said, in a tone of pleased surprise. 'He is an Oxford man,' he added confidently: and we were both deeply interested to know it." The play toured for several months, was revived for the 1888–89 season, and became a Christmas staple for the next four decades.

Writing on the theater

The *Alice* operetta at last gave Dodgson the legitimate role he craved in the theatrical world. Happily immersed and surrounded by his young actress friends, he wrote an essay, "Alice on the Stage," for *The Theatre* in 1887, explaining the origins of the *Alice* story and its characterizations. Later that year he was drawn into a public controversy on the employment of children in the theater. He wrote a letter to the *St. James's Gazette,* and later an essay in the *Times* (London) and *The Theatre,* defending child actors and rejecting the argument that the work was too strenuous for them. He was convinced that theatrical life could be physically, intellectually, and morally strengthening to children, and that their high spirits proved they were not harmed by it. Furthermore, he asserted, the theater offered one of the few respectable sources of income available to young women. The regulations he proposed for ensuring child actors' welfare were very close to those eventually adopted.

Isa Bowman

Foremost among the new friends that stage productions of *Alice* brought him was young Isa Bowman. She and

Left: in 1898 the Opera Comique in London produced the Clarke operetta and printed this handsome souvenir program. Above: another play, by Emily Prime Delafield, appeared in America during Dodgson's lifetime.

Dodgson had become friends when she performed in the first play made from the book, and then in the revival. She is one of the friends associated with a specific Lewis Carroll book, as Alice Liddell is with *Alice in Wonderland* and Gertrude Chataway with *The Hunting of the Snark*. In fact, the dedicatory poem of *Sylvie and Bruno* is a double acrostic on Isa Bowman's name. As a child in the 1880s Isa visited him at Oxford and Eastbourne, and she wrote a memoir of him in 1899.

Not far into middle age, Dodgson had begun to cast himself as the lean and slippered pantaloon, and by now the mantle of universal uncle was firmly on his shoulders, freeing him, he felt, from the censorious judgment of Victorian moralists. Certainly he was subject in his own lifetime to some comment and suspicion concerning his friendships with young girls, as he is today. He was scrupulous in his relations with the children and their parents, and resented such criticisms. When his sister Mary, in an 1893 letter, expressed concern about possible damage to his reputation from having female guests to stay, he replied with asperity that he found public opinion a worthless test of right and wrong: "If you limit your actions in life to things that *nobody* can possibly find fault with, you will not do much!"

Sylvie and Bruno—the secret is love

Smaller works of note from this period include "Feeding the Mind" and the ingenious

Isa Bowman was the first stage Alice and performed in revivals as well.

Dodgson met the 9-year-old Gertrude Chataway on the Isle of Wight in 1875, while writing *The Hunting of the Snark,* and he included a dedicatory poem to her in the book. He was captivated by her practical use of a sailor's jersey and rolled-up trousers as a bathing suit, and sketched her in this charming swimming attire. She was a bright, self-possessed little girl and their immediate mutual appreciation continued into her adult years. While in her twenties, she came to stay with him at Oxford, reveling in his world of logic and whimsy.

Wonderland Postage-Stamp Case. Published posthumously, "Feeding the Mind" was a lecture written and presented in 1884 when an illness unexpectedly extended Dodgson's stay with Edith Denman Draper, a grown and married child-friend whom he had known since 1864. This charming but serious little piece

The Wonderland
Postage-Stamp Case

EIGHT OR NINE
WISE WORDS
about
Letter-Writing
BY
LEWIS CARROLL.
EMBERLIN AND SON
4, MAGDALEN STREET
OXFORD

29217	/90
(217) sendg, J., a	Ap. 1 (Tu.) *Jones, Mrs.* an as present from self and M white elephant.
(218) grand	do. *Wilkins & Co.* bill piano, £175 10s. 6d.

likened the effect of reading material on the mind to that of food on the body: a healthy diet of books and information is necessary to maintain an agile, capable mind.

Dodgson's principal literary undertaking at this time, however, was *Sylvie and Bruno*. This novel, intended for adults and older children, grew out of a mass of ideas and incidents he had jotted down as they came to him over the years. Many of the adventures of the title characters were developed in tales he had told to children at house parties at Hatfield House, ancestral seat of the Cecil family, beginning in the early 1870s. Unlike most of Dodgson's other books, this one progressed slowly, as he gradually wove his collected snippets into a coherent story. In 1885 the tale was complete enough to warrant an illustrator, and he chose the *Punch* cartoonist Harry Furniss, a flamboyant and comical lecturer as well as artist.

Furniss was less tolerant than Tenniel of Dodgson's imperious control of his work. On the other hand, he enjoyed collaborating with an author who cared so passionately about the illustrations. In an entertaining

The Wonderland Postage-Stamp Case is a small folder with little pockets for stamps. It fits into a cardboard sleeve with a picture of Alice holding the baby on it, which corresponds to one on the folder in which the baby has changed into a pig. On the back the Cheshire Cat disappears. It came with *Eight or Nine Wise Words about Letter-Writing,* a witty essay filled with advice both sensible and eccentric. In it, Dodgson made up a humorous sample page from a *Letter Register,* seen here.

Dodgson's photograph of Robert Cecil, Lord Salisbury, prime minister from 1885 to 1902, with his sons. The Cecil children were the first to hear many of the stories that became *Sylvie and Bruno*.

In this caricature by Harry Furniss the illustrator prevents Dodgson from discovering that he has done

memoir, he makes much of Dodgson's demands on him, but also praises his kindness, generosity, and genius. In particular, the author was anxious about the portrayal of the fairy child Sylvie, who embodied many of his ideas about purity and love. He plagued Furniss with photographs of people with the facial features he wanted for her, and with demands that he go sketch people with a particular right ear or nose. In the end, the model was Furniss's own daughter Dorothy.

no work by pretending, eccentrically, not to allow his work to be seen while in progress.

Sylvie and Bruno and its 1893 sequel, *Sylvie and Bruno Concluded,* are not easy to read. There are three worlds to

keep track of—the real world, Outland, and Fairyland—and two interrelated plots: adult romantic and spiritual affairs in the real world and political intriguing in Outland. The narrator is able to move among these worlds with Sylvie and Bruno, and the three—along with some mirror-image characters and events—tie the stories together. The two books are rambling, tedious, mystical, and occasionally banal, and the first edition did not sell out until 1942. The critics were uniformly dismayed.

But no Lewis Carroll book is without its delights. Here we have the Outlandish Watch, which resets time itself; the magnificent nonsense poem known as "The Mad Gardener's Song," as good as any Dodgson wrote; and useful directions for making Fortunatus's Purse, which contains the wealth of the world (since whatever is outside it is also inside it). Most especially, these books yield many rewards to the reader interested in Charles Dodgson.

Trying to finish *Symbolic Logic*

In the last years of Dodgson's life he turned with ever-deepening interest to the study of logic, a natural point of

Left: Sylvie's locket from *Sylvie and Bruno*, drawn by Alice Havers (the only illustration in the book not by Furniss). Sylvie, angelic and maternal, embodies the ideal of love that Dodgson learned from his mother. Her locket says both "Sylvie will love all" and "All will love Sylvie."

The Kangaroo, Buffalo, and Hippo from *Sylvie and Bruno*.

Dodgson wrote to his cousin Fanny Wilcox in 1891, "Somehow, I never seem to have real *leisure,* now, for letter-writing: and in most of my occupations I have the feeling that I am leaving undone other, and perhaps more important things. In fact, every day I stay on here [at Christ Church], is so much deducted from the time I am *hoping* to give, down at Eastbourne, to hard work at *Sylvie and Bruno Concluded.* And, when that's done, there are plenty of books waiting to be finished! If only I could manage, without annoyance to my family, to get imprisoned for 10 years, 'without hard labour,' and *with* the use of books and writing materials, it would be simply delightful!"

confluence between mathematics and language. His overriding desire was to teach people how to think clearly and he saw *Symbolic Logic* as his most important work, intended to make accessible the essential tools for living a responsible, fulfilled life.

After years of labor, he published the first volume of a projected three in 1896; the remainder was reconstructed and published posthumously in 1977. Today his contributions to logic are appreciated as having been ahead of their time, and admired for the clarity of their exposition.

Dodgson found himself speaking in public more frequently during his last years. He had preached on occasion throughout his life, and in the 1890s he spoke at several children's religious services and at St. Mary's Church in Oxford, at least once on his favorite subject of reverence. He gave lessons in logic and told stories to groups of young people at schools, and demonstrated his "Memoria Technica"—a mnemonic system for remembering dates by converting them into words and then making up a rhymed couplet suitable for the event in question.

He continued to meet new child-friends, and by now his circle comprised several generations of grown children. Little Katie Lewis, daughter of Kate Terry, was now married and had her own baby (who grew up to be the actor John Gielgud). Dodgson occasionally called on Lorina Liddell Skene and her children. He accompanied the actress Dorothea Baird, who later originated the part of Trilby and married Henry Irving's son, backstage to meet Ellen Terry, and invited Terry's grown daughter Edith Craig to tea. A wealth of new and old friends, cultivated with care, had multiplied and endured over

The young actress Dorothea Baird, called Dolly, was another of Dodgson's theatrical friends, and a member of the Henry Irving acting dynasty.

the years. His last trip to the theater, two months before his death, was to see J. M. Barrie's *The Little Minister* with his old friend Gertrude Thomson.

Life, what is it but a dream?

In 1897, at age 65, Dodgson remained mentally, physically, and socially active. He regularly took his 18-mile walk and, on his doctor's advice, bought a Whiteley Exerciser. Home at Guildford for Christmas that year, he was working hard on the second volume of *Symbolic Logic* when he developed a bronchial infection. An illness easily treated today, it proved fatal to him; on 14 January 1898 he died. One of his former students, Ethel Rowell, wrote of him, "The intuitive sympathy and understanding love of children…was the mainspring of the genius both of Lewis Carroll and of Mr. Dodgson."

Fairyland interpreted in a turn-of-the-century Arts and Crafts textile.

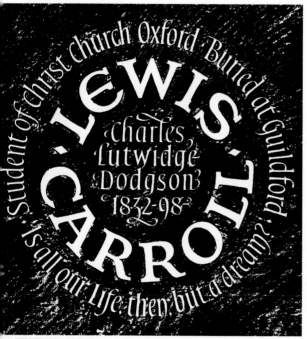

On the sesquicentennial of Dodgson's birth, a stone in his honor was dedicated in the Poet's Corner in Westminster Abbey. Overleaf: Wonderland beckons.

DOCUMENTS

The comic poetry of Lewis Carroll

Dodgson had a lifelong gift for comic poetry; his best works— Alice in Wonderland, Through the Looking-Glass, The Hunting of the Snark— *display a clean, crisp sense of dark humor, and many of his minor poems are equally funny. Even the early works reveal an astonishing facility with language and a recognizably Carrollian voice.*

"My Fairy"

Written by the 13-year-old Charles Dodgson for his family magazine Useful and Instructive Poetry, *this poem, a parody of Victorian instructive rhymes for children, shows that his turn for deadpan irony developed early.*

I have a fairy by my side
    Which says I must not sleep,
When once in pain I loudly cried
    It said "You must not weep."

If, full of mirth, I smile and grin,
    It says "You must not laugh,"
When once I wished to drink some gin,
    It said "You must not quaff."

When once a meal I wished to taste
    It said "You must not bite,"
When to the wars I went in haste,
    It said "You must not fight."

"What may I do?" at length I cried,
    Tired of the painful task,
The fairy quietly replied,
    And said "You must not ask."

    Moral: "You mustn't."

"Disillusionised"

A parody of the popular song "Alice Gray," by William Mee, "Disillusionised" is first cousin to the evidence read in the trial scene of Alice in Wonderland. *It appeared in* College Rhymes *in 1862, and was later retitled "My Fancy."*

I painted her a gushing thing—
    Her years perhaps a score;
I little thought to find them
    At least two dozen more!
My fancy gave her eyes of blue,
    A curling auburn head;

Previous page: the lid of this modern teapot creates the whimsical effect of the Dormouse asleep in the pot.

❝ 'It was much pleasanter at home,' thought poor Alice, 'when one wasn't always growing larger and smaller, and being ordered about by mice and rabbits.… I do wonder what *can* have happened to me!… There ought to be a book written about me, that there ought! And when I grow up, I'll write one—but I'm grown up now,' she added in a sorrowful tone: 'at least there's no room to grow up any more *here*.' ❞ This claustrophobic image is one of Dodgson's own original drawings for *Alice's Adventures under Ground.*

I came to find the blue a green,
    The auburn grown to red!

I painted her a lip and cheek
    In colour like the rose;
I little thought the selfsame hue
    Extended to her nose!
I dreamed of rounded features—
    A smile of ready glee—
But it was not *fat* I wanted,
    Nor a *grin* I hoped to see!

She boxed my ears this morning—
    They tingled very much—
I own that I could wish her
    A somewhat lighter touch:
And if I were to settle how
    Her charms might be improved,
I would not have them added to,
    But just a few removed!

She has the bear's ethereal grace,
    The bland hyena's laugh,
The footstep of the elephant,
    The neck of the giraffe:
I love her still—believe it—
    Though my heart its passion hides;
She's all my fancy painted her,
    But oh! how much besides!

"A Sea Dirge"

Dodgson used the meter of Edgar Allan Poe's celebrated 1849 poem "Annabel Lee" to mock its gloomy tone, bemoaning the miseries of the seaside—in fact a place he loved dearly. This poem was first published in the magazine Temple Bar *in 1862.*

There are certain things—as, a spider, a
    ghost,

The income-tax, gout, an umbrella
   for three—
That I hate, but the thing that I hate
   the most
   Is a thing they call the Sea.

Pour some salt water over the floor—
   Ugly I'm sure you'll allow it to be:
Suppose it extended a mile or more,
   That's very like the Sea.

Beat a dog till it howls outright—
   Cruel, but all very well for a spree:
Suppose that he did so day and night,
   That would be like the Sea.

I had a vision of nursery-maids;
   Tens of thousands passed by me—
All leading children with wooden
   spades,
   And this was by the Sea.

Who invented those spades of wood?
   Who was it cut them out of the tree?
None, I think, but an idiot could—
   Or one that loved the Sea.

It is pleasant and dreamy, no doubt,
   to float
   With 'thoughts as boundless, and
   souls as free':
But suppose you are very unwell in the
   boat,
   How do you like the Sea?

There is an insect that people avoid
   (Whence is derived the verb 'to flee').

Where have you been by it most
   annoyed?
   In lodgings by the Sea.

If you like your coffee with sand for
   dregs,
   A decided hint of salt in your tea,
And a fishy taste in the very eggs—
   By all means choose the Sea.

And if, with these dainties to drink and
   eat,
   You prefer not a vestige of grass or
   tree,
And a chronic state of wet in your feet,
   Then—I recommend the Sea.

For *I* have friends that dwell by the
   coast—
   Pleasant friends they are to me!
It is when I am with them I wonder
   most
   That any one likes the Sea.

They take me a walk: though tired and
   stiff,
   To climb the heights I madly agree;
And, after a tumble or so from the cliff,
   They kindly suggest the Sea.

I try the rocks, and I think it cool
   That they laugh with such an excess
   of glee,
As I heavily slip into every pool
   That skirts the cold cold Sea.

"Hiawatha's Photographing"

*One of Dodgson's cleverest pieces, the
poem excerpted here is a lampoon of
the 1855 Henry Wadsworth Longfellow
verse "The Song of Hiawatha." It first
appeared in* The Train *in 1857. Not
only does it mock Longfellow's tedious
style with great wit, but it also presents a
vivid picture of the photographic portrait*

process of the time. "In an age of imita-
tion [Dodgson writes], I can claim no
special merit for this slight attempt at
doing what is known to be so easy. Any
fairly practised writer, with the slightest
ear for rhythm, could compose, for hours
together, in the easy running metre of
'The Song of Hiawatha.' " Was he right?

From his shoulder Hiawatha
Took the camera of rosewood,
Made of sliding, folding rosewood;
Neatly put it all together.
In its case it lay compactly,
Folded into nearly nothing;
But he opened out the hinges,
Pushed and pulled the joints and
    hinges,
Till it looked all squares and oblongs,
Like a complicated figure
In the Second Book of Euclid.

This he perched upon a tripod—
Crouched beneath its dusky cover—
Stretched his hand, enforcing silence—
Said "Be motionless, I beg you!"
Mystic, awful was the process.

All the family in order
Sat before him for their pictures:
Each in turn as he was taken,
Volunteered his own suggestions,
His ingenious suggestions.

First the Governor, the Father:
He suggested velvet curtains
Looped about a massy pillar;
And the corner of a table,
Of a rosewood dining-table.
He would hold a scroll of something,
Hold it firmly in his left-hand;
He would keep his right-hand buried
(Like Napoleon) in his waistcoat;
He would contemplate the distance
With a look of pensive meaning,
As of ducks that die in tempests.

Grand, heroic was the notion:
Yet the picture failed entirely:
Failed, because he moved a little,
Moved, because he couldn't help it....

Next the Son, the Stunning-Cantab:
He suggested curves of beauty,
Curves pervading all his figure,
Which the eye might follow onward,
Till they centered in the breast-pin,
Centered in the golden breast-pin.
He had learnt it all from Ruskin
(Author of 'The Stones of Venice,'
'Seven Lamps of Architecture,'
'Modern Painters,' and some others);
And perhaps he had not fully
Understood his author's meaning;
But, whatever was the reason,
All was fruitless, as the picture
Ended in an utter failure....

Finally my Hiawatha
Tumbled all the tribe together,
('Grouped' is not the right expression),

An 1883 illustration by Arthur B. Frost for "Hiawatha's Photographing": the Father.

A.B.FROST.

His impenetrable cool has made the Caterpillar appealing to successive generations. In this 1975 poster for Fender electric guitars, he demonstrates an enviable ability to accompany himself on bass.

And, as happy chance would have it,
Did at last obtain a picture
Where the faces all succeeded:
Each came out a perfect likeness.
    Then they joined and all abused it,
Unrestrainedly abused it,
As 'the worst and ugliest picture
They could possibly have dreamed of.
Giving one such strange expressions—
Sullen, stupid, pert expressions.
Really any one would take us
(Any one that did not know us)
For the most unpleasant people!'
(Hiawatha seemed to think so,
Seemed to think it not unlikely).
All together rang their voices,
Angry, loud, discordant voices,
As of dogs that howl in concert,
As of cats that wail in chorus.
    But my Hiawatha's patience,

His politeness and his patience,
Unaccountably had vanished,
And he left that happy party.
Neither did he leave them slowly,
With the calm deliberation
The intense deliberation
Of a photographic artist:
But he left them in a hurry,
Left them in a mighty hurry,
Stating that he would not stand it,
Stating in emphatic language
What he'd be before he'd stand it.
Hurriedly he packed his boxes:
Hurriedly the porter trundled
On a barrow all his boxes:
Hurriedly he took his ticket:
Hurriedly the train received him:
Thus departed Hiawatha.

"The Mad Gardener's Song"

The verses of this splendid poem are scattered throughout the Sylvie and Bruno *books (1889, 1893).*

He thought he saw an Elephant,
    That practiced on a fife:
He looked again, and found it was
    A letter from his wife.
"At length I realize," he said,
    "The bitterness of Life."

He thought he saw a Buffalo
    Upon the chimney-piece:
He looked again, and found it was
    His Sister's Husband's Niece.
"Unless you leave this house," he said,
    "I'll send for the Police!"

He thought he saw a Rattlesnake
    That questioned him in Greek:
He looked again, and found it was
    The Middle of Next Week.
"The one thing I regret," he said,
    "Is that it cannot speak!"

He thought he saw a Banker's Clerk

"Suddenly a kangaroo hopped past her…ka watiwirtjapakanu malu."

A̲bove: a picture from a version of *Alice in Wonderland* set in Australia, illustrated in an Aboriginal art style, and recounted in Pitjantjatjara. Below: an illustration from a Swahili edition. The *Alice* books have been translated into French, Italian, Greek, German, Japanese, Urdu, Frisian, Africaans, Turkish, Croatian, Russian, Serbian, Spanish, Welsh, Irish and Scots Gaelic, Georgian, Bengali, Chinese, Hebrew, Thai, and Lithuanian, among other languages.

It's waiting to be fed!"

He thought he saw an Albatross
　　That fluttered round the lamp:
He looked again, and found it was
　　A Penny-Postage-Stamp.
"You'd best be getting home," he said:
　　"The nights are very damp!"

He thought he saw a Garden-Door
　　That opened with a key:
He looked again and found it was
　　A Double Rule of Three:
"And all its mystery," he said,
　　"Is clear as day to me!"

He thought he saw an Argument
　　That proved he was the Pope:
He looked again, and found it was
　　A bar of Mottled Soap.
"A fact so dread," he faintly said,
　　"Extinguishes all hope!"

Descending from the bus:
He looked again, and found it was
　　A Hippopotamus:
"If this should stay to dine," he said,
　　"There won't be much for us!"

He thought he saw a Kangaroo
　　That worked a coffee-mill:
He looked again, and found it was
　　A Vegetable-Pill.
"Were I to swallow this," he said,
　　"I should be very ill!"

He thought he saw a Coach-and-Four
　　That stood beside his bed:
He looked again, and found it was
　　A Bear without a Head.
"Poor thing," he said, "poor silly thing!

Lewis Carroll the serious poet

Charles Dodgson was eager to speak to his public on serious matters. His introductory poems for Alice in Wonderland *and* Through the Looking-Glass *are poignant reflections, whose air of nostalgia expresses his sentimental side and reveals the influence of Tennyson and Wordsworth. Other poems appeared in periodicals, and some were published in* Phantasmagoria, Rhyme? and Reason?, *and in the collection he was preparing at the time of his death,* Three Sunsets and Other Poems.

"Solitude"

Written in 1853, "Solitude" was the work for which the pseudonym Lewis Carroll *was coined. It first appeared in* The Train.

I love the stillness of the wood:
  I love the music of the rill:
I love to couch in pensive mood
  Upon some silent hill.

Scarce heard, beneath yon arching trees,
  The silver-crested ripples pass;
And, like a mimic brook, the breeze
  Whispers among the grass.

Here from the world I win release,
  Nor scorn of men, nor footstep rude,
Break in to mar the holy peace
  Of this great solitude.

Here may the silent tears I weep
  Lull the vexed spirit into rest,
As infants sob themselves to sleep
  Upon a mother's breast.

But when the bitter hour is gone,
  And the keen throbbing pangs are
    still,
Oh, sweetest then to couch alone
  Upon some silent hill!

To live in joys that once have been,
  To put the cold world out of sight,
And deck life's drear and barren scene
  With hues of rainbow-light.

For what to man the gift of breath,
  If sorrow be his lot below;
If all the day that ends in death
  Be dark with clouds of woe?

Shall the poor transport of an hour
  Repay long years of sore distress—

This 1923 Russian edition of *Alice* not only has a marvelous cover in the Constructivist style, but is a landmark achievement in the art of translation. It was done by a young and pseudonymous Vladimir Nabokov, who was greatly influenced by the book's radical use of language and mixed whimsy and irony.

The fragrance of a lonely flower
   Make glad the wilderness?

Ye golden hours of Life's young spring,
   Of innocence, of love and truth!
Bright, beyond all imagining,
   Thou fairy-dream of youth!

I'd give all wealth that years have piled,
   The slow result of Life's decay,
To be once more a little child
   For one bright summer-day.

"After Three Days"

William Holman Hunt's painting The Finding of the Saviour in the Temple *inspired this poem in the*
Pre-Raphaelite manner, published in Temple Bar *in 1861.*

I stood within the gate
Of a great temple, 'mid the living stream
Of worshipers that thronged its regal
      state
   Fair-pictured in my dream.

Jewels and gold were there;
And floors of marble lent a crystal
      sheen
To body forth, as in a lower air,
   The wonders of the scene.

Such wild and lavish grace
Had whispers in it of a coming doom;
As richest flowers lie strown about the
      face
   Of her that waits the tomb.

The wisest of the land
Had gathered there, three solemn
      trysting-days,
For high debate: men stood on either
      hand
   To listen and to gaze.

The aged brows were bent,
Bent to a frown, half thought, and half
      annoy,
That all their stores of subtlest
      argument
   Were baffled by a boy.

In each averted face
I marked but scorn and loathing, till
      mine eyes
Fell upon one that stirred not in his
      place,
   Tranced in a dumb surprise.

Surely within his mind
Strange thoughts are born, until he
      doubts the lore

Detail from *The Finding of the Saviour in the Temple*, 1854–60.

Of those old men, blind leaders of the
　　blind,
　　Whose kingdom is no more.

　　Surely he sees afar
A day of death the stormy future
　　brings;
The crimson setting of the herald-star
　　That led the Eastern kings.

　　Thus, as a sunless deep
Mirrors the shining heights that crown
　　the bay,
So did my soul create anew in sleep
　　The picture seen by day.

　　Gazers came and went—
A restless hum of voices marked the
　　spot—
In varying shades of critic discontent
　　Prating they knew not what.

　　"Where is the comely limb,
The form attuned in every perfect
　　part,

The beauty that we should desire in
　　him?"
　　Ah! Fools and slow of heart!

　　Look into those deep eyes,
Deep as the grave, and strong with love
　　divine;
Those tender, pure, and fathomless
　　mysteries,
　　That seem to pierce through thine.

　　Look into those deep eyes,
Stirred to unrest by breath of coming
　　strife,
Until a longing in thy soul arise
　　That this indeed were life:

　　That thou couldst find Him there,
Bend at His sacred feet thy willing
　　knee,
And from thy heart pour out the
　　passionate prayer
　　"Lord, let me follow Thee!"

　　But see the crowd divide:
Mother and sire have found their lost
　　one now:
The gentle voice, that fain would seem
　　to chide
　　Whispers "Son, why hast thou"—

　　In tone of sad amaze—
"Thus dealt with us, that art our dearest
　　thing?
Behold, thy sire and I, three weary days,
　　Have sought thee sorrowing."

　　And I had stayed to hear
The loving words "How is it that ye
　　sought?"—
But that the sudden lark, with matins
　　clear,
　　Severed the links of thought.

　　Then over all there fell

Shadow and silence; and my dream was
    fled,
As fade the phantoms of a wizard's cell
    When the dark charm is said.

Yet, in the gathering light,
I lay with half-shut eyes that would not
    wake,
Lovingly clinging to the skirts of night
    For that sweet vision's sake.

"A Song of Love"

The spirit of Sylvie and Bruno *is
expressed in this song, first published in
1893 as the closing of* Sylvie and Bruno
Concluded.

Say, what is the spell, when her
       fledglings are cheeping,
    That lures the bird home to her nest?
Or wakes the tired mother, whose
       infant is weeping,
    To cuddle and croon it to rest?
What the magic that charms the glad
       babe in her arms,
    Till it cooes with the voice of the
    dove?
'Tis a secret, and so let us whisper it
    low—
    And the name of the secret is Love!
      For I think it is Love,
      For I feel it is Love,
    For I'm sure it is nothing but Love!

Say, whence is the voice that, when
       anger is burning,
    Bids the whirl of the tempest to cease?
That stirs the vexed soul with an
       aching—a yearning
    For the brotherly hand-grip of peace?
Whence the music that fills all our
       being—that thrills
    Around us, beneath, and above?
'Tis a secret: none knows how it comes,
    how it goes—

But the name of the secret is Love!
    For I think it is Love,
    For I feel it is Love,
For I'm sure it is nothing but Love!

Say, whose is the skill that paints valley
    and hill,
    Like a picture so fair to the sight?
That flecks the green meadow with
    sunshine and shadow,
    Till the little lambs leap with delight?
'Tis a secret untold to hearts cruel and
    cold,
    Though 'tis sung, by the angels above,
In notes that ring clear for the ears that
    can hear—
    And the name of the secret is Love!
      For I think it is Love,
      For I feel it is Love,
    For I'm sure it is nothing but Love!

The motherly Sylvie comforts Bruno in
Harry Furniss's 1889 drawing.

Letters from Lewis Carroll to his child-friends

Dodgson maintained a correspondence with countless children. A child entertained by an unknown gentleman on a train might soon after receive a letter and a book from Lewis Carroll. Some friendships begun thus continued for years. Many of his child-friends were the children of adult friends, and some were his own nieces and nephews.

To Mary MacDonald

Dodgson was friendly with the entire George MacDonald family for many years, writing, photographing, and visiting them all. Mary was a special favorite. She became engaged to the watercolorist Edward Hughes, but died in 1878 at age 24.

Ch. Ch. Oxford
May 23. 1864.

My Dear Child,

It's been so frightfully hot here that I've been almost too weak to hold a pen, and even if I had been able, there was no ink—it had all evaporated into a cloud of black steam, and in that state it has been floating about the room, inking the walls and ceiling until they're hardly fit to be seen: to-day it is cooler, and a little has come back into the ink-bottle in the form of black snow—there will soon be enough for me to write and order those photographs your Mamma wants.

This hot weather makes me very sad and sulky: I can hardly keep my temper sometimes. For instance, just now the Bishop of Oxford came in to see me—it was a civil thing to do, and he meant no harm, poor man: but I was so provoked at his coming in that I threw a book at his head, which I am afraid hurt him a good deal—(Mem: this isn't quite true—so you needn't believe it—Don't be in such a hurry to believe next time—I'll tell you why—If you set to work to believe everything, you will tire out the believing-muscles of your mind, and then you'll be so weak you won't be able to believe the simplest true things. Only last week a friend of mine set to work to believe Jack-the-giant-killer. He managed to do it, but he was so exhausted by it that when I told him it was raining (which was true) he *couldn't* believe it, but rushed out into the street without his hat or umbrella, the consequence of which was his hair got seriously damp, and one curl didn't recover its shape for nearly two days (Mem: some of *that* is not quite true, I'm afraid—)....

To Dolly Argles

Agnes Argles, known as Dolly, wrote in 1867 to the author of Alice in Wonderland *to ask when there would be a sequel. He responded and soon became a family friend. The object he sent to Dolly's father was a copy of the book* Phantasmagoria.

Ch. Ch. Dec. 11. '68

My Dear Dolly,

...I'm going to send your Papa a little present this Christmas, which I daresay you may like to look at: it consists of some thin slices of dried vegetables that somebody has found a way of preparing so that it doesn't come to pieces easily: they are marked in a sort of pattern with some chemical stuff or other, and fastened between sheets of pasteboard to preserve them. I believe the *sort* of thing isn't a new invention, but the markings of these are quite new: I invented them myself....

To Agnes and Amy Hughes

These were two daughters of Dodgson's friend, the Pre-Raphaelite painter Arthur Hughes. The dates of the letters are unknown.

My Dear Agnes,

You lazy thing! What? I'm to divide the kisses myself, am I? Indeed I won't take the trouble to do anything of the sort! But I'll tell *you* how to do it. First, you take *four* of the kisses, and—that reminds me of a very curious thing that

Alice Liddell Hargreaves in 1932, during a visit to the United States. She had been the first of Dodgson's beloved child-friends.

happened to me at half-past four yesterday. Three visitors came knocking at my door, begging me to let them in. And when I opened the door, who do you think they were? You'll never guess. Why, they were three cats! Wasn't it curious? However, they all looked so cross and disagreeable that I took up the first thing I could lay my hand on (which happened to be the rolling-pin) and knocked them all down as flat as pancakes! "If *you* come knocking at *my* door," I said, "I shall come knocking at *your* heads." That was fair, wasn't it?

Yours affectionately,

Lewis Carroll.

My Dear Agnes,

About the cats, you know. Of course I didn't leave them lying flat on the ground like dried flowers! no, I picked them up, and I was as kind as I could be to them. I lent them the portfolio for a bed—they wouldn't have been comfortable in a real bed, you know: they were too thin—but they were *quite* happy between the sheets of blotting-paper—and each of them had a pen-wiper for a pillow. Well, then I went to bed: but first I lent them the three dinner-bells, to ring if they wanted anything in the night.

You know I have *three* dinner-bells—the first (which is the largest) is rung when dinner is *nearly* ready; the second (which is rather larger) is rung when it is quite ready; and the third (which is as large as the other two put together) is rung all the time I am at dinner. Well, I told them they might ring if they happened to want anything—and, as they rang *all* the bells *all* night, I suppose they did want something or other, only I was too sleepy to attend to them.

In the morning I gave them some rat-tail jelly and buttered mice for breakfast, and they were as discontented as they could be. They wanted some boiled pelican, but of course I knew it wouldn't be good for them. So all I said was "Go to Number Two, Finborough Road, and ask for Agnes Hughes, and if it's *really* good for you, she'll give you some." Then I shook hands with them all, and wished them all goodbye, and drove them up the chimney. They seemed very sorry to go, and they took the bells and the portfolio with them. I didn't find this out till after they had gone, and then I was sorry too, and wished for them back again....

My Dear Amy,
...You asked me after those three cats. Ah! The dear creatures! Do you know, ever since that night they first came, they have *never left me?* Isn't it kind of them? Tell Agnes this. She will be interested to hear it. And they *are* so

kind and thoughtful! Do you know, when I had gone out for a walk the other day, they got *all* my books out of the bookcase, and opened them on the floor, to be ready for me to read. They opened them all at page 50, because they thought that would be a nice useful page to begin at. It was rather unfortunate, though: because they took my bottle of gum, and tried to gum pictures upon the ceiling (which they thought would please me), and by accident they spilt a quantity of it all over the books. So when they were shut up and put by, the leaves all stuck together, and I can never read page 50 again in any of them!

However, they meant it kindly, so I wasn't angry. I gave them a spoonful of ink as a treat: but they were ungrateful for that, and made dreadful faces. But, of course, as it was given them as a treat, they had to drink it. One of them has turned black since: it was a white cat to begin with.

Give my love to any children you happen to meet. Also I send two kisses and a half, for you to divide with Agnes, Emily, and Godfrey. Mind you divide them fairly.

Yours affectionately,
C. L. Dodgson

To Adelaide Paine

The Paines were seaside acquaintances.

Christ Church, Oxford,
March 8, 1880.
My Dear Ada,
(Isn't that your short name? "Adelaide" is all very well, but you see when one is *dreadfully* busy one hasn't time to write such long words—particularly when it takes one half an hour to remember how to spell it—and even then one has to go and get a dictionary to see if one has

spelt it right, and of course the dictionary is in another room, at the top of a high bookcase—where it has been for months and months, and has got all covered with dust—so one has to get a duster first of all, and nearly choke oneself in dusting it—and when one *has* made out at last which is dictionary and which is dust, even *then* there's the job of remembering which end of the alphabet "A" comes—for ones feels pretty certain it isn't in the *middle*—then one has to go and wash one's hands before turning over the leaves—for they've got so thick with dust one hardly knows them by sight—and, as likely as not, the soap is lost, and the jug is empty, and there's no towel, and one has to spend hours and hours in finding things—and perhaps after all one has to go off to the shop to buy a new cake of soap, so, with all this bother, I hope you won't mind my writing it short and saying, "My Dear Ada"). You said in your last letter you would like a likeness of me: so here it is, and I hope you will like it. I won't forget to call the next time but one I'm in Wallington.

Your very affectionate friend,
Lewis Carroll

To Bertie—

This letter is not otherwise identified or dated. It was printed in a collection published by Beatrice Hatch.

The Chestnuts.
Guildford.
June 9

My Dear Bertie,

I would have been very glad to write to you as you wish, only there are several objections. I think, when you have heard them, you will see that I am right in saying 'No'.

The first objection is, I've got no ink—You don't believe it? Ah, you should have seen the ink there was in my days! (About the time of the battle of Waterloo: I was a soldier in that battle). Why, you had only to pour a little of it on the paper, and it went on by itself! *This* ink is so stupid, if you begin a word for it, it can't even finish it by itself.

The next objection is, I've no time. You don't believe *that*, you say? Well, who cares? You should have seen the time there was in *my* days! (At the time of the battle of Waterloo, where I led a regiment). There were always 25 hours in the day—sometimes 30 or 40.

The third and greatest objection is, my great dislike for children. I don't know why, I'm sure: but I *hate* them—just as one hates armchairs and plum-pudding! You don't believe *that*, don't you? Did I ever say you would? Ah, you should have seen the children there were in *my* days! (Battle of Waterloo, where I commanded the English army. I was called 'the Duke of Wellington' then, but I found it a great bother having such a long name, so I changed it to 'Mr. Dodgson'. I chose that name because it begins with the same letter as 'Duke'.) So you see it would never do to write to you.

Have you any sisters? I forget. If you have, give them my love. I am much obliged to your Uncle and Aunt for letting me keep the photograph.

I hope you won't be much disappointed at not getting a letter from

Your affectionate friend,
C. L. Dodgson

To Ethel Hatch

The Hatch family were Oxford friends. Dodgson introduced Ethel to Gertrude Thomson, and she eventually became a professional artist.

Ch. Ch. Mar. 2/84

My Dear Ethel,

Next Tuesday as ever is (a vulgar way of putting it, but never mind!) I've got to dine with Mr. and Mrs. Stewart (you don't know them, but never mind!) in Bradmore Road: time 7.45 (*you* would call it "a quarter to 8" but never mind!) —Now what do you think of this plan! It is an idea of my own, the result of 6 hours of steady thinking.—I could come for you at ½ past 4 (or 5, if that suited you and your lessons better), and fetch you down here (we would take a little walk first, if you wished), give you tea and bread-and-butter at ½ past 5 or 6, show you a picture or so, and fetch you home at ½ past 7: and then I could go on to Bradmore Road and have my dinner. I only ask *you* this time—partly because I've *had* B. and Ethel [He means Evelyn] so very lately (worked 'em off, don't you see? Got rid of 'em. Needn't bother about 'em again for ever-so-long —a vulgar way of putting it, but never mind!), and partly because I like *much* better having children one by one, than two by two, or even forty by forty. Now please don't try and pretend you would like it, if you wouldn't! *Of course* you're a little shy of me: quite natural—You've only to say "I fear I cannot accept your kind invitation, because of the Norman Conquest," I shall quite understand: shan't be offended a bit.

Your very affte.
C.L.D.

To Winifred Stevens

Winifred was one of Dodgson's logic students at Oxford High School. She and her younger sister Edith forged a strong friendship with Dodgson that ended only with his death.

Ch. Ch., May 22, 1887.

My Dear Winnie,

But you will be getting tired of this long letter: so I will bring it to an end, and sign myself,

Yours affectionately,
C. L. Dodgson.

P.S.—I enclose 2 copies of "Castle Croquet."

P.P.S.—You have no idea what a struggle it was to put "Winnie" instead of "Miss Stevens," and "Affectionately" instead of "Yours truly!"

P.P.P.S.—The year after next, or thereabouts, I *hope* to find an opportunity to take you for another walk. By that time, I fear, Time will have begun to write "wrinkles on your azure brow"; however, I don't care! A really *venerable* companion makes one look youthful oneself, and I shall like to hear people whisper to each other, "Who in the world is that *very* interesting-looking boy who is walking with that old lady with snowy tresses, and taking as much care of her as if she were his great-grandmother?"

P.P.P.P.S.—No time for more.

To Violet Dodgson

Violet Dodgson was a niece, the daughter of Dodgson's brother Wilfred.

7 Lushington Road.
Eastbourne.
Aug. 10/92.

My Dear Violet,

A wild idea has just occurred to me— that it is *just* possible you might like to come and stay with me for a few days— I wrote to your father about this idea; and he and your mother have given (though of course *very* reluctantly) their consent— so now all depends on *you*. If your answer to this is "No! No!! No!!!"

Miss Katie R. Terry
from the Author.

Nov. 22/77

ALICE'S ADVENTURES
IN WONDERLAND.

The dedication of a copy of *Alice* to a very special child-friend, Katie Terry, later Lewis, daughter of Kate Terry. Dodgson almost always inscribed his books "from the Author," perhaps to avoid choosing between the names Lewis Carroll and Charles Dodgson. His use of the long "s" in "Miss" was as archaic at the time as it is today.

---

why, then I must write to your parents, and say "the game is up! She turns up her *Noes* at my invitation! And the end of her Noes is (like the end of any *other* Noes) a *snub!* It is humiliating, but I must bear it as well as I can!"

If your answer is "I'd rather *not*: but I don't mind, *just for once,*" why, then I'll fix a day, and come over to Guildford and fetch you. We'll *pretend* that you're going to stay three or four days—though of course I know, well enough, that you'll want to be taken back again the very next day.

Your loving Uncle
Charles L. Dodgson.

To Sydney Bowles

Sydney was the daughter of T. Gibson Bowles, with whom Dodgson corresponded about his word game Syzygies. She grew up to become the mother of the writers Nancy and Jessica Mitford.

Ch. Ch. Oxford
May 22 1891.

My Dear Sydney,

I *am* so sorry, and so ashamed! Do you know, I didn't even know of your *existence*? And it was *such* a surprise to hear that you had sent me your love! It felt just as if Nobody had suddenly run into the room, and given me a kiss! (That's a thing which happens to me, *most* days, just now.) If only I had known you were existing, I would have sent you *heaps* of love, long ago. And, now I come to think about it, I ought to have sent you the love, without being so particular about whether you existed or not. In *some* ways, you know, people that *don't* exist, are much nicer than people that *do*. For instance, people that *don't* exist are never *cross:* and they never *contradict* you: and *they never tread on your toes!* Oh, they're *ever* so much nicer than people that *do* exist! However, never mind; you can't help existing, you know; and I daresay you're *just* as nice as if you didn't.

Which of my books shall I give you, now that I know you're a real child? Would you like 'Alice in Wonderland,' or 'Alice Underground'? (That's the book just as I first wrote it, with my own pictures.)

Please give my love, and a kiss, to Weenie, and Vera, and yourself (don't forget the *kiss* to yourself, please: on the forehead is the best place).

Your affectionate friend,
Lewis Carroll.

The prose of Lewis Carroll

Dodgson wrote some unusual short essays that are not primarily comic, satirical, or professional, and do not address a public controversy. When he had worked something out to his satisfaction he enjoyed sharing it in letters or publications.

Shakespeare nods

Dodgson offered theatrical advice to Ellen Terry on many occasions, not all of it welcome. In this 1880 letter he is concerned not with the fine points of her acting but with a fault he finds in Shakespeare himself—betraying, perhaps, a somewhat naive understanding of the playwright.

…You gave me a treat on Saturday such as I have very seldom had in my life. You must be weary by this time hearing your own praises, so I will only say that Portia was all I could have imagined, and more. And Shylock is superb—especially in the trial-scene.

Now I am going to be very bold, and make a suggestion, which I do hope you will think well enough of to lay before Mr. Irving. I want to see that clause omitted (in the sentence on Shylock)—

That, for this favour,
He presently become a Christian;

It is a sentiment that is entirely horrible and revolting to the feelings of all who believe in the Gospel of Love. Why should our ears be shocked by such words merely because they are Shakespeare's? In his day, when it was held to be a Christian's duty to force his belief on others by fire and sword—to burn man's body in order to save his soul—the words probably conveyed no shock. To all Christians now (except perhaps extreme Calvinists) the idea of forcing a man to abjure his religion, whatever that religion may be, is (as I have said) simply horrible.

I have spoken of it as a needless outrage on religious feeling: but surely, being so, it is a great artistic mistake. Its tendency is directly contrary to the spirit of the scene. We have despised Shylock for his avarice, and we rejoice to see him lose his wealth: we have

H enry Irving as Shylock sometime in the mid- or late 19th century.

abhorred him for his blood-thirsty cruelty, and we rejoice to see him baffled. And now, in the very fulness of our joy at the triumph of right over wrong, we are suddenly called on to see in him the victim of a cruelty a thousand times worse than his own, and to honour him as a martyr. This, I am sure, Shakespeare never meant. Two touches only of sympathy does he allow us, that we may realise him as a man, and not as a demon incarnate. "I will not pray with you"; "I had it of Leah when I was a bachelor." But I am sure he never meant our sympathies to be roused in the supreme moment of his downfall, and, if he were alive now, I believe he would cut out those lines about becoming a Christian.…

Eight or Nine Wise Words about Letter-Writing

The light-hearted but seriously meant essay excerpted here was sold in a packet with the Wonderland Postage-Stamp Case *in 1890. It begins with advice about how best to use the postage-stamp case, and concludes with recommending Dodgson's letter-register system and describing how to set one up.*

§ 3. *How to go on with a Letter*

Here is a golden Rule to begin with. *Write legibly.* The average temper of the human race would be perceptibly sweetened, if every body obeyed this Rule!… Years ago, I used to receive letters from a friend—and very interesting letters too—written in one of the most atrocious hands ever invented. It generally took me about a *week* to read one of his letters! I used to carry it about in my pocket, and take it out at leisure times, to puzzle over the riddles which composed it—holding it in different positions, and at different distances, till at last the meaning of some hopeless scrawl would flash upon me, when I at once wrote down the English under it.…

My second Rule is, don't fill *more* than a page and a half with apologies for not having written sooner!

The best subject, to *begin* with, is your friend's last letter. Write with the letter open before you. Answer his questions, and make any remarks his letter suggests. *Then* go on to what you want to say yourself. This arrangement is more courteous, and pleasanter for the Reader, than to fill the letter with your own invaluable remarks, and then hastily answer your friend's questions in a postscript. Your friend is much more likely to enjoy your wit, *after* his own anxiety for information has been satisfied....

Another Rule is, when you have written a letter that you feel may possibly irritate your friend, however necessary you may have felt it to so express yourself, *put it aside till the next day.* Then read it over again, and fancy it addressed to yourself. This will often lead to your writing it all over again, taking out a lot of the vinegar and pepper, and putting in honey instead, and thus making a *much* more palatable dish of it!...

My seventh Rule is, if it should ever occur to you to write, jestingly, in *dispraise* of your friend, be sure you exaggerate enough to make the jesting *obvious:* a word, spoken in *jest,* but taken as *earnest,* may lead to very serious consequences. I have known it to lead to the breaking off of a friendship. Suppose, for instance, you wish to remind your friend of a sovereign you have lent him, which he has forgotten to repay—you might quite *mean* the words "I mention it, as you seem to have a conveniently bad memory for debts" in jest: yet there would be nothing to wonder at if he took offence at that way of putting it. But, suppose you wrote "Long observation of your career as a pickpocket has convinced me that my only hope, for recovering that sovereign I lent you, is to say 'Pay up, or I'll summons yer!' ", he would indeed be a matter-of-fact friend if he took *that* as seriously meant!...

My tenth Rule. When your letter is finished, read it carefully through, and put in any 'not' that you may chance to have omitted. (This precaution will sometimes save you from saying what

"THE BLUE OF HEAVEN IS LARGER THAN THE CLOUD"
— Browning

Alice's Adventures in Atomland
in the Plastic Age

By
RICHARD M. FIELD

you had not quite intended: *e.g.,* suppose you had *meant* to write "Dear Sir, I am not prepared to accept the offer you make me of your hand and heart.") Then fold up the letter with all the enclosures *in* it, so that all must come out *together.* Otherwise your friend will simply draw out the letter, and put the envelope into the fire, and it will only be when he reaches the words "I enclose £5 bank-note" that he will turn to watch, with tearful gaze, a fragment of white paper-ash, as it flickers up the chimney!

My last Rule. When you take your letters to the Post, *carry them in your hand.* If you put them into your pocket, you will take a long country-walk—I speak from experience—passing the Post-Office *twice,* going and returning, and, when you get home again, will find them *still* in your pocket!

Dodgson's skill at satire inspired many later critics, who have sent a character into a Wonderland to illuminate his follies. *Adolf in Blunderland* (above) was published in 1939, when the British could still find the ambitions and paranoia of Hitler ridiculous. In *Alice's Adventures in Atomland* (opposite), drawn in 1949, the little girl contemplates the apocalypse.

Feeding the Mind

When a sudden illness kept him at the home of his grown and married child-friend Edith Denman Draper, Dodgson made use of the unexpected leisure to write this essay, which he gave as a lecture in 1884. He begins by supposing what would happen if we had conscious control and responsibility for bodily functions, and then extrapolates to the mind:

Well, it is, I say, for us that the body can be clearly seen and felt; and it might be well for some if the mind were equally visible and tangible—if we could take it to the doctor, and have its pulse felt.

'Why, what have you been doing with this mind lately? How have you fed it? It looks pale, and the pulse is very slow.'

'Well, doctor, it has not had much regular food lately. I gave it a lot of sugar-plums yesterday.'

'Sugar plums! What kind?'

'Well they were a parcel of conundrums, sir.'

'Ah, I thought so. Now just mind this: if you go on playing tricks like that, you'll spoil all its teeth, and get laid up with mental indigestion. You must have nothing but the plainest reading for the next few days. Take care now! No novels on any account!'...

I wonder if there is such a thing in nature as a FAT MIND? I really think I have met with one or two: minds which could not keep up with the slowest trot in conversation; could not jump over a logical fence, to save their lives; always got stuck fast in a narrow argument; and, in short, were fit for nothing but to waddle helplessly through the world....

And then, as to the mastication of the food, the mental process answering to this is simply *thinking over* what we read. This is a very much greater exertion of mind than the mere passive taking in the contents of our Author. So much greater an exertion is it, that, as Coleridge says, the mind often 'angrily refuses' to put itself to such trouble—so much greater, that we are far too apt to neglect it altogether, and go on pouring in fresh food on the top of the undigested masses already lying there, till the unfortunate mind is fairly swamped under the flood. But the greater the exertion the more valuable, we may be sure, is the effect. One hour of steady thinking over a subject (a solitary walk is as good an opportunity for the process as any other) is worth two or three of reading only....

Charles Dodgson speaks out

Dodgson often wrote letters to newspapers and published pamphlets on issues under public debate that were close to his heart. He especially hated sloppy thinking and weak logic in argument.

In Defense of Children on the Stage

By the time this letter appeared in The Theatre *in 1889, Dodgson had already spent decades befriending child actors. When a proposal was made to limit or prohibit the employment of children in the theater, on the grounds that it endangered their health and morals, he addressed the question.*

Sir,—I am neither a stage manager nor a dramatic author; I have no children of my own on the stage, or anywhere else; and I have no pecuniary interest in anything theatrical. But I have had abundant opportunities, for many years, for studying the natures of children, including many stage children, and have enjoyed the friendship of many dear children, both on and off the stage.

To these reasons for writing I may, perhaps, be allowed to add that I have given some attention to logic and mathematics, which help so largely in the *orderly* arrangement of topics of controversy—an art much needed when so many controversialists are ladies. Long experience of that delightful sex has taught me that their system of arrangement is that of a circulating decimal, that with them analogy is identity, and reiteration proof, and that they always lay the *onus probandi* on their opponents....

My contention is:—

I. That the employment, in theatres, of children under ten is *not* harmful.

II. That it *is* beneficial.

III. That, while this practice needs certain safeguards not yet provided by the law, it does *not* call for absolute prohibition.

(I.) The harm attributed to this practice may be classed under three headings—(1) physical; (2) intellectual; (3) moral.

(1) "Physical harm."—Take first the charge that it causes "excessive bodily fatigue." To this there was at first an additional item, "enforced by cruelty," which is now practically abandoned, it appearing, on investigation, that no evidence in support of it was forthcoming, while abundant evidence was produced of the kindness such children met with in theatres, and of their thorough enjoyment of their work. According to my experience, the work

The child actress Isa Bowman was a friend of Dodgson from 1888 until his death in 1898.

is well within healthy limits, and the children enjoy it with an intensity difficult to convey by mere words. They like it better than any game ever invented for them. Watch any children you know, in any rank of life, when thrown upon their own resources for amusement, and, if they do not speedily extemporise a little drama, all I can say is that they are not normal children, and they had better see a doctor....

Take, lastly, the gravest and most real of all dangers that come under the category of "moral harm," viz., "the society of profligate men." For adult actresses this danger is, I believe, in well-conducted theatres, distinctly less than it would be in most of the lines of life open to them. Here again the good people, who see such peril in the life of an actress, seem to be living in a fool's paradise, and to fancy they are legislating for young ladies who, if they did not go on the stage, would be secluded in drawing-rooms where none but respectable guests are admitted. Do they suppose that attractive-looking young women, in the class from which the stage is chiefly recruited, would be safer as barmaids or shopwomen from the insidious attentions of the wealthy voluptuary than they are as actresses?

But if it be granted that young women of this class may choose a stage life with as fair a chance of living a reputable life as they would have in any other profession open to them, it is surely desirable to begin learning their business as soon as they are competent, unless it can be shown that they are in greater danger as children than as young women. I believe the danger is distinctly less.

Their extreme youth is a powerful safeguard. To plot evil against a child, in all its innocence and sweet trustfulness and ignorance of the world, needs no common voluptuary; it needs one so selfish, so pitiless, and so abject a coward as to be beneath one calling himself a man.

II. My second contention is that stage life is beneficial to children, even the youngest; and this in three ways— (1) physically, (2) intellectually, and (3) morally.

(1) Physically. The deportment that must be acquired for even moderately good acting, and the art of dancing, which most stage children acquire, not only give grace of figure and of action, but are excellent for the health. In girls' schools, not so many years ago, spinal curvature was so common than an eminent surgeon, Dr. Mayo, put it on record that scarcely three per cent escaped it. I am glad to believe that they are more sensibly managed now, and that the days are passed away when it was "vulgar" for young ladies to run, and where the only bodily exercise allowed them was to walk two-and-two; but I feel sure that, even now, if one hundred children were taken at random from the highly educated classes, and another hundred from the stage, the latter would show a better average for straightness of spine, strength, activity, and the bright, happy look that tells of health. The stage child "feels its life in every limb"—a locality where the Board school child feels only its lessons.

(2) Intellectually. Comparing children with children, my belief is that stage life distinctly *brightens* the mind of a child. Of course the same result is produced at schools, whenever they can manage to *interest* the pupils in their work. But how often they fail to do this! How often are the poor little victims made to do work "against the grain"! And all such work is not only badly done, but is intensely fatiguing and depressing to spirits and intellect alike.

(3) Morally. I believe that stage life, in a well-conducted theatre, is valuable moral training for young children. They learn—

(*a*) Submission to discipline.

(*b*) Habits of order and punctuality.

(*c*) Unselfishness (this on the principle on which you always find children in large families less selfish than only children).

(*d*) Humility. This because, however clever they may think themselves, they soon find out that others are cleverer....

He suggests the imposition of some regulations, including minimum ages, licencing, and maximum hours, and concludes:

But I do not believe that the law can absolutely prohibit children under ten from acting in theatres without doing a cruel wrong to many a poor struggling family, to whom the child's stage salary is a godsend, and making poor children miserable by debarring them from a healthy and innocent occupation which they dearly love....

Some Popular Fallacies about Vivisection

While not especially an animal lover, Dodgson was a compassionate person and always concerned with humankind's quest to develop and express a better nature. Vivisection, like Darwinism, was one of

The fairy-child Sylvie weeps for a dead hare in an 1889 illustration by Harry Furniss. Dodgson protested against the inhumane treatment of animals as a question of morality.

the hotly argued scientific and moral questions of the day.

At a time when this painful subject is engrossing so large a share of public attention, no apology, I trust, is needed for the following attempt to formulate and classify some of the many fallacies, as they seem to me, which I have met with in the writings of those who advocate the practice. No greater service can be rendered to the cause of truth, in this fiercely contested field, than to reduce these shadowy, impalpable phantoms into definite forms, which can be seen, which can be grappled with, and which, when once fairly *laid,* we shall not need to exorcise a second time.

I begin with two contradictory propositions, which seem to constitute the two extremes, containing between them the golden mean of truth—

1. *That the infliction of pain on animals is a right of man, needing no justification.*

2. *That it is in no case justifiable.*

The first of these is assumed in practice by many who would hardly venture to outrage the common feelings of humanity by stating it in terms. All who recognize the difference of right and wrong must admit, if the question be closely pressed, that the infliction of pain is in *some* cases wrong. Those who deny it are not likely to be amenable to argument. For what common ground have we? They must be restrained, like brute beasts, by physical force.

The second has been assumed by an Association lately formed for the total suppression of Vivisection, in whose manifesto it is placed in the same category with Slavery, as being an absolute evil, with which no terms can be made. I think I may assume that the proposition most generally accepted is an intermediate one, namely, that the infliction of pain is in some cases justifiable, but not in all.…

Here he separates the right to inflict pain from the right to inflict death, asserting that we could not take a walk for fear of crushing insects if we had no right at all to kill animals.

4. *That man is infinitely more important than the lower animals, so that the infliction of animal suffering, however great, is justifiable if it prevent human suffering, however small.*

This fallacy can be assumed only when unexpressed. To put it into words is almost to refute it. Few, even in an age where selfishness has almost become a religion, dare openly avow a selfishness so hideous as this! While there are thousands, I believe, who would be ready to assure the vivisectors that, so far as their personal interests are concerned, they are ready to forego any prospect they may have of a diminution of pain, if it can only be secured by the infliction of so much pain on innocent creatures.

But I have a more serious charge than that of selfishness to bring against the scientific men who make this assumption. They use it dishonestly, recognizing it when it tells in their favour, and ignoring it when it tells against them. For does it not presuppose the axiom that human and animal suffering differ *in kind*? A strange assertion this, from the lips of people who tell us that man is twin-brother to the monkey! Let them be at least consistent, and when they have proved that the lessening of the *human* suffering is an end so great and glorious as to justify any means that will secure it, let them give the anthropomorphoid ape the benefit of the argument. Further than that I will not ask them to go, but will resign them in confidence to the guidance of an exorable logic.

Had they only the candour and the courage to do it, I believe they would choose the other horn of the dilemma, and would reply, "Yes, man *is* in the same category as the brute; and just as we care not (you see it, so we cannot deny it) how much pain we inflict on the one, so we care not, unless when deterred by legal penalties, how much we inflict on the other. The lust for scientific knowledge is our real guiding principle. The lessening of human suffering is a mere dummy set up to amuse sentimental dreamers."…

6. *That the pain inflicted on an individual animal in vivisection is not greater than in sport.*

I am no sportsman, and so have no right to dogmatize, but I am tolerably sure that all sportsmen will agree with me that this is untrue of shooting, in which, whenever the animal is killed at once, it is probably as painless a form of death as could be devised; while the sufferings of one that escapes wounded ought to be laid to the charge of unskilful sport, not of sport in the abstract. Probably much of the same might be said of fishing: for other forms of sport, and especially for hunting, I have no defense to offer, believing that they involve very great cruelty....

He then makes his chief point:

We see this most clearly, when we shift our view from the act itself to its remoter consequences. The hapless animal suffers, dies, "and there an end": but the man whose sympathies have been deadened, and whose selfishness has been fostered, by the contemplation of pain deliberately inflicted, may be the parent of others equally brutalized, and so bequeath a curse to future ages. And even if we limit our view to the present time, who can doubt that the degrada-tion of a soul is a greater evil than the suffering of bodily frame?...[Quoting a newspaper article,] "...the testimony of an English physiologist...may be useful in conclusion. He was present some time past at a lecture, in the course of which demonstrations were made on living dogs. When the unfortunate creatures cried and moaned under the operation, many of the students *actually mimicked their cries in derision!* The gentleman who related this occurrence adds that the spectacle of the writhing animals and the fiendish behavior of the audience so sickened him, that he could not wait for the conclusion of the lecture, but took his departure in disgust."

It is a humiliating but an undeniable truth, that man has something of the wild beast in him, that a thirst for blood can be aroused in him by wit-nessing a scene of carnage, and that the infliction of torture, when the first instincts of horror have been deadened by the familiarity may become, first a matter of indifference, then a subject of morbid interest, then a positive pleasure, and then a ghastly and ferocious delight....

Dodgson is not impressed with the stated motives of vivisectors.

It is my conviction that the non-scientific world is far too ready to attribute to the advocates of science all the virtues they are so ready to claim; and when they put forward their favourite *ad captandum* argument that their labours are undertaken for one pure motive—the good of humanity—society...is far too ready to accept the picture of the pale, worn devotee of science giving his days and nights to irksome and thankless toil, spurred on by no other motive than a boundless philanthropy. As one who has himself devoted much time and labour to scientific investigations, I desire to offer the strongest possible protest against this falsely coloured picture. I believe that any branch of science, when taken up by one who has a natural turn for it, will soon become as fascinating as sport to the most ardent sportsman, or as any form of pleasure to the most refined sensualist. The claim that hard work, or the endurance of privation, proves the existence of an unselfish motive, is simply monstrous....

Dodgson concludes that selfishness lies at the root of the practice of vivisection, and of the indifference of the general public to it, based on another fallacy:

13. *That the practice of vivisection will never be extended so as to include human subjects.*

That is, in other words, that while science arrogates to herself the right of torturing at her pleasure the whole sentient creation up to man himself, some inscrutable boundary line is there drawn, over which she will never venture to pass....And surely the easygoing Levites of our own time would take an altogether new interest in this matter, could they only realize the possible advent of a day when anatomy shall claim as legitimate subjects for experiment, first, our condemned criminals—next, perhaps, the inmates of our refuges for incurables—then the hopeless lunatic, the pauper hospital-patient, and generally "him that hath no helper"—a day when successive generations of students, trained from their earliest years to the repression of all human sympathies, shall have developed a new and more hideous Frankenstein—a soulless being to whom science shall be all in all....

The New Belfry of Christ Church, Oxford

The renovations made to the Great Quadrangle occasioned a number of Dodgson's publications on Christ Church and Oxford business. Here he mocks the mannerisms of scholarship to make his point.

§ 1. *On the etymological significance of the new Belfry, Ch. Ch.*

The word "Belfry" is derived from the French *bel,* "beautiful, becoming, meet," and from the German *frei,* "free, unfettered, secure, safe." Thus the word is strictly equivalent to "meat-safe," to which the new Belfry bears a resemblance so perfect as almost to amount to coincidence.

§ 2. *On the style of the new Belfry, Ch. Ch.*

The style is that which is usually

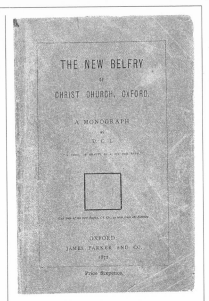

The cover of Dodgson's 1872 critique of the new belfry of Christ Church Cathedral. The "east view" of the belfry, as illustrated in the *blank* square, was in Dodgson's opinion the best perspective.

known as "Early Debased": very early, and remarkably debased.

§ 3. *On the origin of the new Belfry, Ch. Ch.*

...The head of the House, and the architect, feeling a natural wish that their names should be embodied, in some conspicuous way, among the alterations then in progress, conceived the beautiful and unique idea of representing, by means of a new Belfry, a gigantic copy of a Greek Lexicon [The architect was Sir George Gilbert Scott; thus this reference to the famous Liddell-Scott Greek Lexicon.]. But, before the idea had been reduced to a working form, business took them both to London for a few days, and during their absence, somehow (*this* part of the business has never been satisfactorily explained) the whole thing was put into the hands of a wandering architect, who gave the name of Jeeby. As the poor man is now incarcerated at Hanwell, we will not be too hard upon his memory, but will only say that he professed to have originated the idea in a moment of inspiration, when idly contemplating one of those highly coloured, and mysteriously decorated chests which, filled with dried leaves from gooseberry bushes and quickset hedges, profess to supply the market with tea of genuine Chinese growth. Was there not something prophetic in the choice? What traveller is there, to whose lips, when first he enters that great educational establishment and gazes on its newest decoration, the words do not rise unbidden—"Thou tea-chest"?…

§ 4. *On the chief architectural merit of the new Belfry, Ch. Ch.*

Its chief merit is its Simplicity—a Simplicity so pure, so profound, in a word, so *simple,* that no other word will fitly describe it. The meagre outline, and baldness of detail, of the present Chapter, are adopted in humble imitation of this great feature.

§ 5. *On the other architectural merits of the new Belfry, Ch. Ch.*

The Belfry has no other architectural merits.

§ 6. *On the means of obtaining the best views of the new Belfry, Ch. Ch.*

The visitor may place himself, in the first instance, at the opposite corner of the Great Quadrangle, and so combine, in one grand spectacle, the beauties of the North and West sides of the edifice. He will find that the converging lines forcibly suggest a vanishing point, and if that vanishing point should in its turn suggest the thought, "would that *it* were on the point of vanishing!" he may perchance, like the Soldier in the Ballad, "lean upon his sword" (if he has one: they are not commonly worn by modern tourists), "and wipe away a tear."…

The *best* view of the Belfry is that selected by our Artist for the admirable frontispiece which he has furnished for the first Volume of the present work. This view may be seen, in all its beauty, from the far end of Merton Meadow. From that point the imposing position (or, more briefly, the imposition) of the whole structure is thrillingly apparent. There the thoughtful passer-by, with four right angles on one side of him, and four anglers, who have no right to be there, on the other, may ponder on the mutability of human things, or recall the names of Euclid and Isaac Walton, or smoke, or ride a bicycle, or do anything that the local authorities will permit.

§ 7. *On the impetus given to Art in England by the new Belfry, Ch. Ch.*

The idea has spread far and wide, and is rapidly pervading all branches of manufacture. Already an enterprising maker of bonnet-boxes is advertising "the Belfry pattern": two builders of bathing machines at Ramsgate have followed his example: one of the great London houses is supplying "bar-soap" cut in the same striking and symmetrical form: and we are credibly informed that Borwick's Baking Powder and Thorley's Food for Cattle are now sold in no other shape.…

Selections from the *Sylvie and Bruno* books

As works of literature, Sylvie and Bruno *and* Sylvie and Bruno Concluded *must be considered interesting failures. They are unique and original, the manifestation of one of Dodgson's defining qualities: an indomitable individualism that kept him always true to his vision, in large things and small. However, they are also all but unreadable. While the* Alice *books can be enjoyed by both children and adults, the* Sylvie and Bruno *books do not particularly appeal to either. For the reader interested in Dodgson's feelings and ideas, though, they are a treasure.*

The secret of enjoying life

Charles Dodgson believed in doing everything deliberately.

The old man sighed. "And so it is," he said, "look at it as you will. Life is indeed a drama; a drama with but few *encores*—and no *bouquets!*" he added dreamily. "We spend one half of it in regretting the things we did in the other half!"

"And the secret of *enjoying* it," he continued, resuming his cheerful tone, "is *intensity!*…What I mean is intensity of *thought*—a concentrated *attention*. We lose half the pleasure we might have in Life, by not really *attending*. Take any instance you like: it doesn't matter *how* trivial the pleasure may be—the principal is the same. Suppose *A* and *B* are reading the same second-rate circulating-library novel. *A* never troubles himself to master the relationships of the characters, on which perhaps all the interest of the story depends: he 'skips' over all the descriptions of scenery, and every passage that looks rather dull: he doesn't half attend to the passages he does read: he goes on reading—merely from want of resolution to find another occupation—for hours after he ought to have put the book aside: and reaches the 'FINIS' in a state of utter weariness and depression! *B* puts his whole soul *into* the thing—on the principle that 'whatever is worth doing is worth doing *well*': he masters the genealogies: he calls up pictures before his 'mind's eye' as he reads about the scenery: best of all, he resolutely shuts the book at the end of some chapter, while his interest is yet at its keenest, and turns to other subjects; so that, when next he allows himself an

Mein Herr shows Lady Muriel how to make Fortunatus's Purse, in Harry Furniss's 1893 illustration.

hour at it, it is like a hungry man sitting down to dinner: and, when the book is finished, he returns to the work of his daily life like 'a giant refreshed'!"

"But suppose the book were really *rubbish*—nothing to repay attention?"

"Well, suppose it," said the Earl. "My theory meets *that* case, I assure you! *A* never finds out that it *is* rubbish, but maunders on to the end, trying to believe he's enjoying himself. *B* quietly shuts the book, when he's read a dozen pages, walks off to the Library, and changes it for a better!"

Sylvie and Bruno

Fortunatus's Purse

Dodgson imagines a version of the Klein Bottle, *the three-dimensional counterpart of the* Moebius Strip.

"You have heard of Fortunatus's Purse, Miladi? Ah, so! Would you be surprised to hear that, with three of these leetle handkerchiefs, you shall make the Purse of Fortunatus, quite soon, quite easily?"

"Shall I indeed?" Lady Muriel eagerly replied, as she took a heap of them into her lap, and threaded her needle. "*Please* tell me how, Mein Herr! I'll make one before I touch another drop of tea!"

"You shall first," said Mein Herr, possessing himself of two of the handkerchiefs, spreading one upon the other, and holding them up by two corners, "you shall first join together these upper corners, the right to the right, the left to the left; and the opening between them shall be the *mouth* of the Purse."

A very few stitches sufficed to carry out *this* direction. "Now, if I sew the other three edges together," she suggested, "the bag is complete?"

"Not so, Miladi: the *lower* edges shall *first* be joined—ah, not so!" (as she was beginning to sew them together). "Turn one of them over, and join the *right* lower corner of the one to the *left* lower corner of the other, and sew the lower edges together in what you would call *the wrong way*."

"*I* see!" said Lady Muriel, as she deftly executed the order. "And a very twisted, uncomfortable, uncanny-looking bag it makes! But the *moral* is a lovely one. Unlimited wealth can only be attained by doing things *in the wrong way!* And how are we to join up these mysterious—no, I mean *this* mysterious opening?" (twisting the thing round and round with a puzzled air.) "Yes, it *is* one opening. I thought it was *two*, at first."

"You have seen the puzzle of the Paper Ring?" Mein Herr said, addressing the Earl. "Where you take a slip of paper, and join its ends together, first twisting one, so as to join the *upper* corner of *one* end to the *lower* corner of the *other?*"

"I saw one made, only yesterday," the Earl replied. "Muriel, my child, were you not making one, to amuse those children you had to tea?"

"Yes, I know that Puzzle," said Lady Muriel. "The Ring has only *one* surface, and only *one* edge. It's very mysterious!"

"The *bag* is just like that, isn't it?" I suggested. "Is not the *outer* surface of one side of it continuous with the *inner* surface of the other side?"

"So it is!" she exclaimed. "Only it *isn't* a bag, just yet. How shall we fill up this opening, Mein Herr?"

"Thus!" said the old man impressively,

taking the bag from her, and rising to his feet in the excitement of the explanation. "The edge of the opening consists of *four* handkerchief-edges, and you can trace it continuously, round and round the opening: down the right edge of *one* handkerchief, up the left edge of the *other*, and then down the left edge of the *one*, and up the right edge of the *other!*"

"So you can!" Lady Muriel murmured thoughtfully, leaning her head on her hand, and earnestly watching the old man. "And that *proves* it to be only *one* opening!"…

"Now, this *third* handkerchief," Mein Herr proceeded, "has *also* four edges, which you can trace continuously round and round: all you need do is join its four edges to the four edges of the opening. The Purse is then complete, and its outer surface—"

"I see!" Lady Muriel eagerly interrupted. "Its *outer* surface will be continuous with its *inner* surface! But it will take time. [It will of course also take a fourth dimension.—ed.] I'll sew it up after tea." She laid aside the bag, and resumed her cup of tea. "But why do you call it Fortunatus's Purse, Mein Herr?"

The dear old man beamed upon her, with a jolly smile.…"Don't you see, my child—I should say Miladi? Whatever is *inside* that Purse, is *outside* it; and whatever is *outside* it, is *inside* it. So you have all the wealth of the world in that leetle Purse!"

Sylvie and Bruno Concluded

Wagering as morally elevating

Dodgson lived according to strict moral precepts. He did not, however, subscribe to any received notions of what might be innately moral or immoral.

"I *never* bet," she sternly replied.

"Not even sixpenny points at *whist?*"

"*Never!*" she repeated. "*Whist* is innocent enough: but whist played for *money!*" She shuddered.

Arthur became serious again. "I'm afraid I ca'n't take that view," he said. "I consider that the introduction of small stakes for card-playing was one of the most *moral* acts Society ever did, *as* Society."

"How was it so?" said Lady Muriel.

"Because it took Cards, once for all, out of the category of games at which *cheating* is possible. Look at the way Croquet is demoralising Society. Ladies are beginning to cheat at it, terribly: and, if they're found out, they only laugh, and call it fun. But when there's *money* at stake, that is out of the question. The swindler is *not* accepted as a wit. When a man sits down to cards, and cheats his friends out of their money, he doesn't get much *fun* out of it—unless he thinks it fun to be kicked down stairs!"

Sylvie and Bruno Concluded

The fallacies of teetotalism

Dodgson saw neither gambling nor drinking as evil in themselves; rather, he despised excess as a form of vice, and disliked received opinions.

So Lady Muriel took up the cudgels. "Do you hold the theory," she enquired, "that people can preach teetotalism more effectually by being teetotalers themselves?"

"Certainly I do!" replied the red-faced man. "Now, here is a case in point," unfolding a newspaper-cutting: "let me read to you this letter from a teetotaler. *To the Editor. Sir, I was once a moderate drinker, and knew a man who*

drank to excess. I went to him. 'Give up this drink,' I said. 'It will ruin your health!' 'You drink,' he said: 'why shouldn't I?' 'Yes,' I said, 'but I know when to leave off.' He turned away from me. 'You drink in your way,' he said: 'let me drink in mine. Be off!' Then I saw that, to do any good with him, I must forswear drink. From that hour I haven't touched a drop!'

"There! What do you say to *that?*" He looked round triumphantly, while the cutting was handed round for inspection.

"How very curious!" exclaimed Arthur, when it had reached him. "Did you happen to see a letter, last week, about early rising? It was strangely like this one."

The red-faced man's curiosity was roused. "Where did it appear?" he asked.

"Let me read it to you," said Arthur. He took some papers from his pocket, opened one of them, and read as follows. *To the Editor. Sir, I was once a moderate sleeper, and knew a man who slept to excess. I pleaded with him. 'Give up this lying in bed,' I said, 'It will ruin your health!' 'You go to bed,' he said: 'why shouldn't I?' 'Yes,' I said, 'but I know when to get up in the morning.' He turned away from me. 'You sleep in your way,' he said: 'let me sleep in mine. Be off!' Then I saw that to do any good with him, I must forswear sleep. From that hour I haven't been to bed!'*

Arthur folded and pocketed his paper, and passed on the newspaper-cutting. None of us dared to laugh, the red-faced man was evidently so angry. "Your parallel doesn't run on all fours!" he snarled.

"*Moderate* drinkers never do so!" Arthur quietly replied.

Sylvie and Bruno Concluded

A selection from *The Hunting of the Snark*

The darkly humorous poem The Hunting of the Snark, *billed as "An Agony in Eight Fits," was published on April Fool's Day in 1876. The following passages introduce the strange crew and their even more peculiar quarry.*

FIT THE FIRST
THE LANDING

"Just the place for a Snark!" the
    Bellman cried,
  As he landed his crew with care;
Supporting each man on the top of the
    tide
  By a finger entwined in his hair.

"Just the place for a Snark! I have said it
    twice:
  That alone should encourage the crew.
Just the place for a Snark! I have said it
    thrice:
  What I tell you three times is true."

The crew was complete: it included a
    Boots—
  A maker of Bonnets and Hoods—
A Barrister, brought to arrange their
    disputes—
  And a Broker, to value their goods.

A Billiard-marker, whose skill was
    immense,
  Might perhaps have won more than
    his share—
But a Banker, engaged at enormous
    expense,
  Had the whole of their cash in his
    care.

There was also a Beaver, that paced on
    the deck,
  Or would sit making lace in the bow:
And had often (the Bellman said) saved
    them from wreck,
  Though none of the sailors knew how.

There was one who was famed for the
    number of things
  He forgot when he entered the ship:
His umbrella, his watch, all his jewels
    and rings,

Henry Holiday, the original illustrator of *The Hunting of the Snark* in 1876, draws the Snark-hunters on board their ship.

And the clothes he had bought for
    the trip.

He had forty-two boxes, all carefully
    packed,
    With his name painted clearly on
    each:
But since he omitted to mention the
    fact,
    They were all left behind on the
    beach.

The loss of his clothes hardly mattered,
    because
    He had seven coats on when he came,
With three pairs of boots—but the
    worst of it was,
    He had wholly forgotten his name.

He would answer to "Hi!" or to any
    loud cry,
    Such as "Fry me!" or "Fritter my
    wig!"
To "What-you-may-call-um!" or
    "What-was-his-name!"
    But especially "Thing-um-a-jig!"

While, for those who preferred a more
    forcible word,
    He had different names from these:
His intimate friends called him
    "Candle-ends,"
    And his enemies "Toasted-cheese."

"His form is ungainly—his intellect
    small—"
    (So the Bellman would often
    remark)—
"But his courage is perfect! And that,
    after all,
    Is the thing that one needs with a
    Snark."

He would joke with hyenas, returning
    their stare
    With an impudent wag of the head:
And he once went a walk, paw-in-paw,
    with a bear,
    "Just to keep up its spirits," he said.

He came as a Baker: but owned, when
    too late—
    And it drove the poor Bellman half-
    mad—
He could only bake Bride-cake—for
    which, I may state,
    No materials were to be had.

The last of the crew needs especial
    remark,
    Though he looked an incredible
    dunce:
He had just one idea—but, that one
    being "Snark,"

A bathing-machine of the sort Snarks like, drawn by Jonathan Dixon in a 1992 edition.

The good Bellman engaged him at once.

He came as a Butcher: but gravely declared,
    When the ship had been sailing a week,
He could only kill Beavers. The Bellman looked scared,
    And was almost too frightened to speak:

But at length he explained, in a tremulous tone,
    There was only one Beaver on board;
And that was a tame one he had of his own,
    Whose death would be deeply deplored.

The Beaver, who happened to hear the remark,
    Protested, with tears in its eyes,
That not even the rapture of hunting the Snark
    Could atone for this dismal surprise!…

FIT THE SECOND
THE BELLMAN'S SPEECH

…"Friends, Romans, and countrymen, lend me your ears!"
    (They were all of them fond of quotations:
So they drank to his health, and they gave him three cheers,
    While he served out additional rations).

"We have sailed many months, we have sailed many weeks,
    (Four weeks to the month you may mark).
But never as yet ('tis your Captain who speaks)

Have we caught the least glimpse of a
   Snark!
"We have sailed many weeks, we have
   sailed many days,
   (Seven days to the week I allow),
But a Snark, on the which we might
   lovingly gaze,
   We have never beheld till now!

"Come, listen, my men, while I tell you
   again
   The five unmistakable marks
By which you may know, wheresoever
   you go,
   The warranted genuine Snarks.

"Let us take them in order. The first is
   the taste,
   Which is meagre and hollow, but
   crisp:
Like a coat that is rather too tight in the
   waist,
   With a flavour of Will-o-the-Wisp.

"Its habit of getting up late you'll
   agree
   That it carries too far, when I say
That it frequently breakfasts at five-
   o'clock tea,
   And dines on the following day.

"The third is its slowness in taking a
   jest.
   Should you happen to venture on
   one,
It will sigh like a thing that is deeply
   distressed:
   And it always looks grave at a pun.

"The fourth is its fondness for bathing-
   machines,
   Which it constantly carries about,
And believes that they add to the
   beauty of scenes—
   A sentiment open to doubt.

"The fifth is ambition. It next will be
   right
   To describe each particular batch:
Distinguishing those that have feathers,
   and bite,
   From those that have whiskers, and
   scratch.

"For although common Snarks do no
   manner of harm,
   Yet I feel it my duty to say
Some are Boojums—" The Bellman
   broke off in alarm,
   For the Baker had fainted away.

As Lewis Carroll he is famous for his wit and marvelous facility with language, as Charles L. Dodgson for his sensitive, discerning photographs. The man's love of art and literature, his talent for the mechanics of photography and the logical processes of mathematics were facets of his complex personality. This gentle portrait of his friend the painter Arthur Hughes with his young daughter Agnes captures another salient element of Dodgson's character: the value he placed on family affection.

Chronology

1832 Charles Lutwidge Dodgson born in Daresbury, Cheshire, England, January 27

1843 Family moves to Croft Rectory, Yorkshire

1844–45 Attends Richmond Grammar School, Warwick

1846–49 Attends Rugby School

1850 Matriculates at Christ Church, Oxford

1851 Takes up residence at Christ Church in January. Mother dies

1852 Becomes a student (Fellow) of Christ Church, a lifetime privilege to live in rooms at Christ Church and receive a small stipend

1854 Receives a Bachelor of Arts degree with First Class Honors in Mathematics and Second Class Honors in Classics. Begins to publish verse

1855 Becomes Mathematical Lecturer at Christ Church (until 1881). Begins to attend the theater in London

1856 First uses the pseudonym Lewis Carroll in print, in the magazine *The Train*. Meets Alice Liddell. Buys photographic equipment

1857 Becomes Sub-Librarian at Christ Church

1861 Ordained deacon of the Church of England

1862 On a river outing, July 4, with Alice, her sisters, and friends, tells the *Alice* story

1865 *Alice in Wonderland* is published in July but is withdrawn due to faulty printing; new edition published in November, dated 1866

1867 Travels to Germany and Russia with his friend Henry Liddon.

Publishes "Bruno's Revenge"

1868 Father dies. Family moves to Guildford. Dodgson moves to his last set of rooms at Christ Church

1869 Publishes *Phantasmagoria*

1871 Publishes *Through the Looking-Glass* in December, dated 1872

1876 Publishes *The Hunting of the Snark*

1877 First of many summer visits to seaside Eastbourne

1879 Publishes *Euclid and His Modern Rivals*

1880 Takes his last known photograph

1881 Resigns Mathematical Lectureship

1882 Elected Curator of the Christ Church Senior Common Room

1885 Publishes *A Tangled Tale*

1886 Publishes facsimile edition of *Alice's*

Adventures under Ground. Henry Savile Clarke's theatrical adaptation of *Alice in Wonderland* is produced in London

1887 Publishes *The Game of Logic*

1889 Publishes *Sylvie and Bruno*

1890 Publishes *The Nursery Alice* and issues the Wonderland Postage-Stamp Game

1892 Resigns Common Room curatorship

1893 Publishes *Sylvie and Bruno Concluded*

1896 Publishes *Symbolic Logic, Part I*

1898 Dies of bronchitis, January 14, two weeks before his 66th birthday. *Three Sunsets and Other Poems*, already at printer, is published. Buried in Guildford

Further Reading

BOOKS BY LEWIS CARROLL / CHARLES L. DODGSON

A Syllabus of Plane Algebraical Geometry, 1860

Alice's Adventures in Wonderland, 1865, [1866]

An Elementary Treatise on Determinants, 1867

Phantasmagoria, 1869

Though the Looking-Glass, and What Alice Found There, 1871, [1872]

Euclid, Book V, 1874

Euclid, Books I, II, 1875

The Hunting of the Snark, An Agony in Eight Fits, 1876

Doublets, 1879

Euclid and His Modern Rivals, 1879

Rhyme? and Reason?, 1883

A Tangled Tale, 1885

Alice's Adventures under Ground, 1886

The Game of Logic, 1886, [1887]

Curiosa Mathematica Part I: A New Theory of Parallels, 1888

Sylvie and Bruno, 1889

The Nursery Alice, 1889

Curiosa Mathematica Part II: Pillow Problems Thought Out during Sleep, 1893

Sylvie and Bruno Concluded, 1893

Symbolic Logic, Part I, 1896

Three Sunsets and Other Poems, 1898 (posthumous)

ON LEWIS CARROLL, CHARLES L. DODGSON, AND HIS WORLD

Abeles, Francine F. (ed.), *The Mathematical Pamphlets of Charles Lutwidge Dodgson and Related Pieces*, 1994

Almansi, Guido (ed.), *Lewis Carroll: Photos and Letters to His Child Friends*, 1975

Aspin, Roy, *Lewis Carroll and His Camera*, 1989

Auerbach, Nina, *Ellen*

Terry: Player in Her Time, 1987

Bartley, W. W., III (ed.), *Lewis Carroll's 'Symbolic Logic,'* 1977

Bill, E. G. W., and J. F. A. Mason, *Christ Church and Reform, 1850–1867,* 1970

Bowman, Isa, *The Story of Lewis Carroll Told for Young People by the Real Alice in Wonderland,* 1899

Clark, Anne, *Lewis Carroll: A Biography,* 1979

————, *The Real Alice: Lewis Carroll's Dream Child,* 1981

Cohen, Morton N., *Lewis Carroll: A Biography,* 1995

———— (ed.), *The Letters of Lewis Carroll,* 1979

———— (ed.), *Lewis*

Carroll: Interviews and Recollections, 1989

Cohen, Morton N., and Anita Gandolfo (eds.), *Lewis Carroll and the House of Macmillan,* 1987

Collingwood, Stuart Dodgson, *The Life and Letters of Lewis Carroll,* 1898

Engel, A. J., *From Clergyman to Don: The Rise of the Academic Profession in Nineteenth Century Oxford,* 1983

Gardner, Martin (ed., intro., and notes), *The Annotated Alice,* 1960

————, *More Annotated Alice,* 1990

Gernsheim, Helmut, *Lewis Carroll: Photographer,* 1949

Green, Roger Lancelyn (ed.), *The Diaries of Lewis Carroll,* 1953

Guiliano, Edward (ed.), *Lewis Carroll: A Celebration,* 1982

———— (ed.) *Lewis Carroll Observed,* 1976

Guiliano, Edward, and James R. Kincaid (eds.), *Soaring with the Dodo: Essays on Lewis Carroll's Life and Art,* 1982

Hancher, Michael, *The Tenniel Illustrations to the "Alice" Books,* 1985

Hatch, Evelyn M. (ed.), *A Selection from the Letters of Lewis Carroll to His Child-Friends,* 1933

Hinde, Thomas (ed.), *Looking-Glass Letters,* 1991

Hudson, Derek, *Lewis*

Carroll: An Illustrated Biography, rev. ed., 1976

Liddon, Henry Parry, *The Russian Journal II,* ed. by Morton N. Cohen, 1979

Lovett, Charles C., *Alice on Stage,* 1990

Phillips, Robert (ed.), *Aspects of Alice,* 1972

Terry, Ellen, *The Story of My Life,* 1908

Wakeling, Edward (ed.), *The Oxford Pamphlets, Leaflets, and Circulars of Charles Lutwidge Dodgson,* 1993

Weaver, Warren, *Alice in Many Tongues,* 1964

Williams, Sidney Herbert, Falconer Madan, and Roger Lancelyn Green, *The Lewis Carroll Handbook,* 1962

List of Illustrations

Key: ***a***=above; ***b***=below; ***c***=center; ***l***=left; ***r***=right

Abbreviations: AW=*Alice's Adventures in Wonderland* (various editions of the book); GC=Gernsheim Collection, Harry Ransom Humanities Research Center, The University of Texas at Austin; NA=*The Nursery Alice,* first edition, London: Macmillan, 1889; PUL=Princeton University Library, Morris L. Parrish Collection, Department of Rare Books and Special Collections, Princeton, N.J.; RML=Rosenbach Museum & Library, Philadelphia, Pa.; SB=*Sylvie and Bruno,* first edition, London:

Macmillan, 1889; SBC=*Sylvie and Bruno Concluded,* first edition, London: Macmillan, 1893; TLG=*Through the Looking-Glass, and What Alice Found There* (various editions of the book)

Front cover Illustration of Lewis Carroll altered using a photograph by O. G. Rejlander of Charles L. Dodgson with a camera lens, 1863. GC (detail of page 12). Color illustrations by John Tenniel, NA (details). **Spine** Detail of a color illustration by John Tenniel, NA, 1889 **Back cover** John Tenniel, color illustration, NA, 1889

1 Charles L. Dodgson, photograph of Alice Liddell as a beggar-child, probably late 1850s. PUL
2 Charles L. Dodgson, photograph of Florence Bickersteth, 1865. GC
3, 4 John Tenniel, illustrations for AW (London: Macmillan), 1865 [1866]
5 Charles L. Dodgson, photograph of Arthur Hughes, Jr., 12 October 1863. GC
6 John Tenniel, illustration for TLG (London: Macmillan), 1871 [1872]
7 Charles L. Dodgson, photograph of Dymphna Ellis, c. 1865. GC
8 John Tenniel, illustration for TLG (London: Macmillan), 1871 [1872]
9 Charles L. Dodgson,

photograph of Xie Kitchin as a Chinaman on Tea Boxes, 14 July 1873. GC
11 John Tenniel, illustration for a 1946 Random House, New York, special edition of AW, colored by Fritz Kredel
12 O. G. Rejlander, photograph of Charles L. Dodgson, 1863. GC
13 John Tenniel, color illustration, NA, 1889
14l Charles Dodgson, Sr., date and photographer unknown; from Stuart Dodgson Collingwood, *The Life and Letters of Lewis Carroll* (London: T. Fisher Unwin), 1898
14r James McNeill Whistler, *Harmony in Green and Rose: The Music Room,* 1860–61, oil on

Index

Page numbers in italics refer to captions and/or illustrations.

A

Adam and Eve (Rembrandt), *95*
Adolf in Blunderland, *149*
"After Three Days," 51, 137–39
Alice (character), *80, 81, 99, 107*, in *Alice in Wonderland*, 3, 6, 59, *59, 64*, 65, *68*, 68–72, *69, 70, 71, 131*; in *Through the Looking-Glass, 96, 97*, 97–99, *98*
Alice in Wonderland, 22, 35, 59, *64*, 64–80, 85, 91, *104*, 110, 121, 136, *149*; facsimile edition, 80, *80–81*, 83, 116, 119; first editions, *79*, 79–80; illustrations of characters, *2–9, 13, 29, 62, 67–77, 134, see also* Alice (character); international editions, *68, 70, 135, 137*; Macmillan and, 72, 76–77, 78, 90; staging, 49, *118*, 118–20, *119, 120*, 121, *121*
Alice in Wonderland, a Dream Play for Children, 119, 119–20, *120*
"Alice on the Stage," 106, 120
Alice's Adventures in Atomland, 148, 149
Alice's Adventures under Ground, 66, *66*, 67, 77, *130*
"Alice Statue," *82*
All the Year Round, 35
American Telegrams, 86

Appleton, D., 79
Argles, Dolly, 141
Arnold, Ethel and Julia, 104–5
Arnold, Matthew, 93, 104
At the Back of the North Wind (MacDonald), 67
Aunt Judy's Magazine, 101, 102, *104*

B

Baird, Dorothea, 126, *126*
Behind the Looking-Glass, 95
Bertie, 143
Blue and Gold: The Rose Azalea (Whistler), *92*
Bond, Anne Lydia, *40*
Boughton, Alice, 46, *46*
Bowles, Sydney, 145
Bowles, T. Gibson, 145
Bowman, Isa, 120–21, *121, 151*
Brine, Katie, *41, 44*
British Museum, *60*, 80, *81*
"Bruno's Revenge," 99, *101*, 102, *102*

C

Cameron, Julia Margaret, 36, 46, *47*, 117
Carlo, Phoebe, 118, *119*
Carnation, Lily, Lily, Rose (Sargent), *58, 59*
Carroll, Lewis. *See* Dodgson, Charles Lutwidge
Cassatt, Mary, *40, 41*
Cecil family, 122, *123*
Chataway, Gertrude, 121, *121*
Cheshire, 14
Chestnuts, The, 94
Children—Nude (Boughton), *46*

Clarke, Henry Savile, 118, *118, 119, 120*
Coleridge, Samuel Taylor, 27
Collingwood, Stuart Dodgson, 16–17
Combe, Thomas, 76
Comic Times, 32
Coote, Bert, 48
Craig, Edith, 126
Croft, 15–16, 94
Crystal Palace, *22–23*, 23
Cunnynghame, Maggie, 25
Curiosa Mathematica II: Pillow Problems, 115, *116*

D

Dadd, Richard, *54*
D'Alcourt, Dorothy, *119*
Daresbury, 14
Davy and the Goblin, 78
Delafield, Emily Prime, *120*
Dickens, Charles, 35
"Difficulties No. I," 21
"Disillusionised," 86–87, 130–31
Disraeli, Benjamin, *98*
Dixon, Jonathan, *164*
Dodgson, Charles Lutwidge, *12, 13, 24, 25, 66*; animals and, 103–4, 152–56, *153*; appearance, 30, 35; birth, 14; as Lewis Carroll, 14, 32–34, 57, 70, 105, 107, 112, 118, 121, 127, *165*, character, 17, 25, 40–41, 46, 55, 96, *108, 109*, 136, *145, 165*; child actors and, 120, 150–52; child-friends, 16, 36, 37–39, 40–41, 46–48, 57, 60–66, *82–83*, 87, 90, 104–5,

111–12, *112*, 121, *121*, 122, 126–29, 140–45; child-hood, 14–18, *19*; Christ Church and, *22*, 22–32, *26, 28, 29*, 54–57, *71*, 86, 91, 94, 102, 103, *113*, *125*, 156–57, *157*; as curator, 116–17; death, 127; education, 15, 16–18, 22–25; family magazines, 18–22, 27, 130; letter writing, 110, 146–48; lifestyle, 27, 57, *85*, 104–5, 107, 109, 110–11, *125*, 127; mathematics and, 26–27, 29, 54–55, 86, *90*, 90–91, *110*, 111, 113, 115, *116, 165*; parents, 14–15, 22, 25, *93*, 93–94; photography and, 23, 32, 35–46, 57, 60, *88, 89, 90, 94, 105*, 113–14, *114, 165*; as poet, 18–19, 33–35, 57, 86–87, 102–3, *103*, 105–7, 130–39; religion and, 56–57, 91–93; sexuality and, 46–48; siblings, 14, 16, 94, 105, *105*; stammering of, 20, 30–31, 46, 56, *56, 57, 63*, 67; as teacher, 25–32; theater and, 48–50, 56, *57*, 87, 90, 92, 117–20, *126*, 127, 150–52
Dodgson, Charles, Sr., *14*, 15, 22, 25, *93*, 93–94
Dodgson, Edwin, *16*
Dodgson, Elizabeth, 63
Dodgson, Fanny, 62
Dodgson, Mary, 105, 121
Dodgson, Violet, 144–45
Dodgson, Wilfred, 105, 144
dodo, *60*, 61, *63*
Doublets, 111

Acknowledgments

The author is especially grateful to John Campbell of the Wonderland Press for suggesting and developing this project; to Toula Ballas, Paul Gottlieb, Adrienne Moucheraud, and Eve Sinaiko of Harry N. Abrams, Inc., for their enthusiasm and support; to Morton N. Cohen and Anne Clark Amor for their guidance and invaluable body of work; and to Charles Lovett for opening the doors. For their assistance in making available valuable photographs, thanks are due to Alice Clark of the Parrish Collection at Princeton University, David Coleman of the Harry Ransom Humanities Research Center at the University of Texas at Austin, Elizabeth Fuller and Stephen Urice of the Rosenbach Museum & Library in Philadelphia, and David and Maxine Schaefer. The author also thanks her family, Judge Stoffel and Lucy Lovett, for their love and encouragement.

Photograph Credits

Stephanie Lovett Stoffel is a scholar and collector of the
works of Lewis Carroll. She has co-authored *Lewis Carroll's
Alice,* a bibliographical checklist of the Lovett Collection,
holds a master's degree in English literature from
Wake Forest University, and serves on the board of
the Lewis Carroll Society of North America.

For Harry N. Abrams, Inc.
Series manager: Eve Sinaiko
Typographic designer: Elissa Ichiyasu
Design Supervisor: Tina Thompson
Cover designer: Dana Sloan
Permissions: Barbara Lyons

Library of Congress Cataloging-in-Publication Data

Stoffel, Stephanie Lovett, 1962–
    Lewis Carroll in Wonderland : the life and times of Alice and her creator /
Stephanie Lovett Stoffel.
        p.   cm. — (Discoveries)
    Includes bibliographical references and index.
    ISBN 0–8109–2838–8
    1. Carroll, Lewis, 1832–1898—Biography.   2. Authors, English—19th
century—Biography.   3. Mathematics teachers—England—Oxford—Biography.
4. Mathematicians—Great Britain—Biography.   5. Photographers—Great
Britain—Biography.   I. Title.   II. Series: Discoveries (New York, N.Y.)
    PR4612.S78   1997
    828'.809—dc21
    [B]   96–39346

Copyright © 1997 The Wonderland Press, New York
Published in 1997 by Harry N. Abrams, Inc., New York
Editorial content developed by the Wonderland Press, New York

Lewis Carroll in Wonderland: The Life and Times of Alice and Her Creator
is part of the Découvertes (Discoveries) series, conceived, developed, and produced by
Editions Gallimard Jeunesse, Paris

Printed and bound in Italy by Editoriale Libraria, Trieste